WELSH PLACE NAMES

THEIR MEANINGS EXPLAINED

by

E. M. H. Davies, B.A. (Hons)
Welsh, Dip. Ed.

First Published, 1978
Revised and Reprinted, 1979

ISBN 0 907453 09 0

Printed by Qualitex Printing Ltd., Cardiff

Price 65p

PREFACE

Place names in Wales provide a fascinating study. Most of the names are descriptive of their locations. An understanding of what the name means is often a vital clue to knowing the place itself. This book is a short guide to the meanings of place names from all over Wales.

Most Welsh places also have an English name. In some cases this is merely a corrupt version of the original Welsh name (e.g. Llanfair Isgoed has produced Llanvair Discoed). In other cases the English name is totally unrelated to the Welsh name (e.g. Abertawe and Swansea). A list of English names has therefore been given separately in an appendix at the end of the book.

Pronunciation of the Welsh names may prove difficult for the visitor. The main sounds which differ from English are as follows:–

- a – as in *are* (long vowel) or as in *tram* (Short vowel).
- ch – as in the Scottish *loch*.
- dd – as 'th' in *this*.
- e – as 'a' in *mane* (long vowel) or as 'e' in *ten* (short vowel).
- f – as the English 'v'
- ff – as the English 'f'
- g – always hard, as in *gate*.
- ll – the tongue is positioned to form an 'l' but the breath is pushed out without using the voice.
- r – rolled more strongly than in English.
- rh – both the 'r' and 'h' should be pronounced.
- th – as in *both*.
- u – as 'ee' in *feet* (long vowel) or as 'i' in *it* (short vowel).
- w – as 'oo' in pool (long vowel) or as 'oo' in book (short vowel).
- y – as 'ee' in *deed* (long vowel) or as 'i' in *pin* (short vowel).

The letters K, Q, V, X and Z do not occur in Welsh and these sounds are conveyed by other letters or diphthongs.

CONTENTS

I COMMON PREFIXES IN WELSH PLACE NAMES

Some prefixes, or stems, appear time and again in Welsh place names.

Aber – this denotes the mouth of a river, a small stream, or the confluence of a river. It is usually followed by the name of the river. Examples are:–

Abercraf – mouth of the river Craf (= garlic).
Abernant – mouth of a stream.
Aberllynfi – mouth of the river Llynfi (= smooth).

Betws – a house of prayer. This is usually followed by the location of the prayer house or by its founder's name. Examples are:–

Betws y Coed – prayer house in the wood.
Betws Garmon – prayer house of Garmon.
Betws Ifan – prayer house of Evan.

Blaen – the source of a river or the head of a valley. (Blaenau is the plural form). Examples are:–

Blaen-bedw – source of the river Bedw (= birch trees).
Blaen-cwm – head of the valley. This is a village situated at the head of the Rhondda valley.
Blaenau Ffestiniog – heads of the valleys in the land of Ffestin.

Bryn – a hill.

Brynarian – hill of silver.
Brynhyfryd – pleasant hill.
Bryncastell – castle hill.

Bwlch – a pass or gap.

Bwlch-mawr – big pass.
Bwlch y Ddau Faen – pass of the two stones.
Bwlch y Mynydd – mountain pass.

Capel – a chapel.

Capel Dewi – chapel of David, the patron Saint of Wales.
Capel Seion – chapel of Zion.
Capel Newydd – new chapel.

Castell a castle.

Castell Pictwn – Picton's castle.
Castell Coch – red castle
Castell Maen – stone castle

Coed – a wood.
Coed-y-bryn – wood of the hill.
Coed-yr-Ystrad – wood of the vale.
Coed-y-brenin – King's wood.

Cwm – a shallow valley.
Cwm-bach – a small valley.
Cwm Hirnant – valley of the long stream.
Cwm Elái – valley of the Elái river.

Dan – below (also Tan)
Dan-y-coed – below the wood.
Dan-y-graig – below the rock.
Tanygrisiau – below the steps.

Eglwys – a church.
Eglwys-fach – little church.
Eglwys y Drindod – Trinity church.
Eglwys Wen – White church.

Esgair – a ridge.
Esgairdawe – ridge of the river Tawe (= quiet).
Esgair Hirnant – ridge of the long stream.
Esgair Ddu – black ridge.

Ffridd – a mountain pasture or sheep-walk.
Ffridd Fawr – big mountain pasture.
Ffridd y Foel – mountain pasture of the bare hill.
Ffriddisaf – lower mountain pasture.

Ffynnon – a well or spring.
Ffynnongroyw – clear spring or well.
Ffynnon Taf – Taf's well.
Ffynnon-bedr – St. Peter's well.

Gelli – a grove.
Gelli-aur – golden grove.
Gellilydan – wide grove.
Gellifelen – yellow grove.

Glan – a river or water bank.
Glan-llyn – the bank of a lake.
Glan-y-don – bank or shore of the wave.
Glanyrafon – bank of the river.

Glyn – a glen or valley.
Glynteg – fair glen.
Glynebwy – glen of the river Ebwy.
Glyncorrwg – glen of the two Corrwg streams.

Gors – from Cors, meaning a bog, fen or marsh.
Gors Lydan – wide marsh.
Gorseinon – the fen of Einion.
Gors-goch – red marsh.

Hafod – a summer dwelling or summer pasture.
Hafod yr Ynys – summer dwelling of the island.
Hafod-wen – fair summer dwelling or pasture.
Hafod Fraith – mottled summer pasture.

Llan – a church. This is usually followed by the name of the saint to whom the church is dedicated..
Llanddewi – Church of St. David.
Llanbadrig – Church of St. Patrick.
Llanfair – Church of St. Mary.
(Llan- may also refer to a parish).

Llwyn – a bush or grove.
Llwyn-onn – ash grove.
Llwynypia – bush of the magpie.
Llwyndyrys – tangled grove.

Llyn – a lake or pool.
Llyn Helyg – lake of the willows.
Llyn Hywel – Hywel's lake.
Llyn Hir – long lake.

Maes – a field or plain.
Maes-glas – green field.
Maes-y- bont – field of the bridge.
Maes-y-crugiau – field of the cairns.

Moel – a bare hill.
Moel Garegog – rocky, bare hill.
Moel Sych – dry, bare hill.
Moel y Llyn – bare hill of the lake.

Mynydd – a mountain.
Mynydd Coch – red mountain.
Mynydd Uchaf – highest mountain.
Mynydd Margam – Morgan's mountain.

Nant – a stream.
Nantglyn – stream of the glen.
Nant-y-pandy – stream of the fulling mill.
Nantgarw – rough stream.

Pant – a hollow or valley.
Pantycelyn – hollow of the holly trees.
Pant yr Ynn – hollow of the ash trees.
Pantysgallog – hollow of thistles.

Pen – top or end.
Pen-twyn – top of the hill.
Penrhos – end of the moorland.
Pentraeth – end of the beach.

Pentre – a village.
Pentre Isaf – lower village.
Pentre'r Felin – village of the mill.
Pentre Bont – village of the bridge.

Pont – a bridge.
Pont Siân – Siân's bridge.
Pontaman – bridge over the river Aman.
Pontgarreg – bridge of stone.

Pwll – a pool or pit.
Pwll-glâs – blue pool.
Pwll-y-glaw – the rain pool.
Pwll defaid – sheep's pool or pit.

Rhiw – a slope or hillside.
Rhiwlas – green slope.
Rhiwderyn – bird's hillside.
Rhiw Cilgwyn – hill of the white nook.

Rhos – moorland.
Rhos-yr-hafod – moorland of the summer dwelling.
Rhosbwlch – moorland of the pass.
Rhos-goch – red moorland.

Rhyd – a ford or stream.
Rhyd-y-foel – ford of the bare hill.
Rhydfach – little ford.
Rhyd-ddu – black ford.

Tal – end or front.
Tal-y-bont – end of the bridge.
Talgarreg – end or front of the rock.
Talerddig – end of the little garden.

Tre – a homestead or town (also Tref).
Treffynnon – homestead of the well.
Trefecca – homestead of Becca.
Trefdraeth – homestead or town of the beach.

Tŷ – a house.
Tyddewi – house of St. David.
Tŷ-hen – old house.
Tŷ-newydd – new house.

Tyn – (from Tyddyn) – a small holding.
Tyn-y-pwll – small holding of the pool.
Tyn-cwm – small holding in the valley.
Tyn-y-Pistyll – small holding near the well or spring.

Waun – (from Gwaun) – moorland or meadow.
Waun Fawr – large meadow.
Waun Lwyd – grey meadow or moorland.
Waunarlwydd – lord's meadow.

Ystrad – a wide bottomed valley.
Ystradmynach – monk's valley.
Ystradowen – Owen's valley.
Ystradyfodwg – valley of St. Tyfodwg.

II PLACE NAMES IN CLWYD

Abergele –	mouth of the river Gele.
Allt Tairffynnon –	hillside or wood of three wells.
Babell –	tent or pavillion.
Bangor Is-coed –	Bangor below the wood.
Betws Gwerful Goch –	prayer house of Gwerful the red.
Betws-yn-Rhos	prayer house in the moorland.
Bontnewydd –	new bridge.
Bontuchel –	high bridge.
Bryn Du –	black hill.
Bryneglwys –	hill of the church.
Brynffordd –	hill of the road.
Brynsaithmarchog –	hill of seven Knights.

Bryn Trillyn – hill of three pools or lakes.
Bryn-y-maen – hill of the stone.
Bwlch-gwyn – white pass.
Bylchau – passes or gaps.
Cadair Fronwen – the chair of Bronwen.
Castell y Rhodwydd – castle of the ford or embankment.
Castell y Waun – castle of the moor.
Cefn – ridge.
Cefn-brith – mottled ridge.
Cefn-bychan – little ridge.
Cefn Du – black ridge.
Cefn-mawr – large ridge.
Cefn Treffynnon – ridge of the homestead of the well.
Cefn-y-bedd – ridge of the grave.
Cerrig Coediog – woody rocks.
Cerrigydrudion – rocks of the brave ones.
Cilcain – beautiful retreat.
Clawddnewydd – new bank.
Coedgolau – light wood.
Coed-poeth – warm wood.
Corwen – boulder denoting a sacred place.
Craig y Forwyn – maiden's rock.
Craig yr Ychen – the oxen's rock.
Cwm Pennant – valley of the head of the stream.
Derwen – oak tree.
Diserth – winderness.
Foel Frech – bare, speckled hill.
Foel Goch – bare red hill.
Foel Wen – bare white hill.
Ffridd Fawr – large mountain pasture.
Ffridd y Foel – mountain pasture of the bare hill.
Ffynnongroyw – clear well or spring.
Garn Fawr – large cairn.
Garth – enclosure or headland.
Gelliöedd – groves.
Glan-y-don – shore of the wave.
Glanyrafon – bank of the river.
Glasfryn – green hill
Glyndyfrdwy – glen of the river Dyfrdwy.
Gorsedd – throne.
Gorsedd Brân – throne of Brân (a character from the Mabinogion-Welsh folklore).
Graeanrhyd – gravelly ford.
Graig – rock.
Graigfechan – little rock.
Groesffordd – crossroads.

Gwernymynydd –	marsh of the mountain.
Gwynfryn –	white hill.
Hen Graig –	old rock.
Henllan –	old church.
Is-y-coed –	below the wood.
Llanbedr Dyffryn Clwyd –	church of St. Peter in the Clwyd valley.
Llanddulas –	church on the river Dulas.
Llanfair Dyffryn Clwyd –	church of St. Mary in the Clwyd valley.
Llanfynydd –	church of the mountain.
Llangwm –	church of the valley.
Llannerch-y-môr –	glade of the sea..
Llansanffraid Glynceiriog –	St. Bridget's church in the glen of (the river) Ceiriog.
Llan San Sior –	church of St. George.
Llanynys –	church of the island.
Llanypwll –	church of the pool or pit.
Llwyn-mawr –	large grove.
Llysbedydd –	court of christening or baptism.
Llysfaen –	court of stone.
Maes-gläs –	green field.
Melin-y-wig –	mill of the wood.
Mochdre –	homestead of pigs.
Moelfre –	bare hill.
Moelfre-isaf –	lower bare hill.
Moelfre-uchaf –	upper bare hill.
Moel Garegog –	stony bare hill.
Moel Geraint –	bare hill of Geraint.
Moel Llyn –	bare hill of the lake.
Moel Llys-y-coed –	bare hill of the court of the wood.
Moel Morfudd –	bare hill of Morfudd.
Moel Plas-yw –	bare hill of the mansion of the yew trees.
Moel Tywysog –	bare hill of the prince.
Moel y Gaer –	bare hill of the fort.
Moel yr Henfaes –	bare hill of the old field.
Morfa Caer –	sea-marsh of the fort.
Mynydd-isa –	lower mountain.
Mynydd Maesyrychen –	the mountain of the oxen's field.
Mynydd Rhyd-ddu –	mountain of the black ford.
Mynydd Tarw –	bull mountain.
Nantglyn –	stream of the glen.
Oernant –	cold stream.
Pandy –	fulling mill.

Pandy'r Capel — fulling mill of the chapel.
Pandytudur — Tudor's fulling mill.
Penmaen-rhos — head of the rock of the moor.
Pentre — village.
Pentre-bach — little village.
Pentrecelyn — village of the river Celyn (holly).
Pentre-dŵr — village of water.
Pentrefoelas — village of the bare green hill.
Pentre-isaf — lower village.
Pentre'r felin — village of the mill.
Pen-y-cae — end or top of the field.
Pen-y-cefn — end of the ridge.
Pen-y-ffordd — end of the road.
Penymynydd — top of the mountain.
Pen yr Eryr — head of the eagle.
Pen yr Orsedd — top of the throne.
Plas Llwyd — grey mansion.
Pontfadog — bridge of Madog.
Pwll-glas — blue pool.
Rhiwlas — green hillside.
Rhosllannerchrugog — moorland of the heathery glade.
Rhosrobin — moorland of the robin.
Rhuddlan — red church.
Rhydlydan — wide ford.
Rhyd-y-foel — ford of the bare hill.
Rhyd-y-Meudwy — ford of the hermit.
Sycharth — dry enclosure.
Tai-bach — small houses.
Talwrn — rocky place.
Tan-y-fron — below the hillside.
Tanypistyll — below the well or spring.
Traeth Gwyn — white beach.
Trefalun — homestead of Alun.
Trefechan — little homestead.
Trefnant — homestead of the stream.
Treffynnon — homestead of the well.
Tŷ-nant — house of the stream.
Tyn-y-pwll — smallholding of the pool or pit.
Y Cwm — the valley.
Y Fron — the hillside.
Y Fron Deg — the fair hillside.
Y Groes — the cross.
Y Maerdy — the dairy house or the steward's house.
Y Parlwr Du — the black parlour.
Y Waun — the moorland.

III PLACE NAMES IN DYFED

Aberaeron – mouth of the river Aeron (fruits or berries).
Aberarth – mouth of the river Arth (a bear).
Aber-cuch – mouth of the river Cuch (frown).
Aberdaugleddau – mouth of the two Cleddy rivers –
Cleddy Ddu (black or Eastern Cleddau).
Cleddy Wen (white or Western Cleddau).
Aber–ffrwd – mouth of a stream.
Abergorlech – mouth of the river Gorlech (sloping or rocky).
Abergwaun – mouth of the river Gwaun (meadow or moor).
Aber Gwendraeth – mouth of the river Gwendraeth (white shore).
Abergwili – mouth of the river Gwili.
Aber-nant – mouth of a stream.
Aberteifi – mouth of the river Teifi.
Aberystwyth – mouth of the river Ystwyth (flexible).
Alltwalis – hillside of the Wallis.
Allt-y-coed – hillside of the wood.
Allt-yr-hebog – wood of the hawk.
Amroth – near the mound.
Babel – Biblical name.
Bae Abergwaun – the bay of the mouth of the Gwaun river.
Bae Caerfyrddin – the bay of the fort of Myrddin.
Bae Ceredigion – the bay of the land of Ceredig.
Bae Sant Ffraid – the bay of St. Bridget.
Bae Trefdraeth – the bay of the homestead of the shore.
Bancffosfelen – bank of the yellow ditch or brook.
Banc Melyn – yellow mound.
Banc Nant – bank of a stream,
Bancycapel – hillside of the chapel.
Bancyfelin – hillside of the mill.
Banc-y-moelfre – mound of the bare hill.
Bethania – biblical name (Bethany).
Bethlehem – biblical name.
Betws Bledrws – the house of prayer of Bledrws.
Betws Ifan – the prayer house of Evan.
Blaenannerch – source of the river Annerch (greeting).
Blaen-ffos – source of a brook.
Blaenhafren – source of the river Hafren (the Severn).
Blaenpennal – source of he river Pennal.
Blaen-plwyf – head of the parish.
Blaen-porth – head of the gateway or harbour.
Blaen-waun – head of the moorland or meadow.
Blaen-y-coed – head of the wood.

Boncath –	a buzzard.
Borth Uchaf –	upper harbour.
Brechfa –	mottled place.
Bronnant –	hillside of the stream.
Bronwydd –	hillside of trees.
Bryn –	a hill.
Brynaman –	hill of the river Aman.
Brynberian –	hill of Berian.
Bryn Cysegr-lân –	hill of the holy sanctuary.
Bryn Dafydd –	David's hill.
Bryn Du –	black hill.
Bryn Garw –	rough hill.
Brynhenllan –	hill of the old church.
Bryn Hir-faen –	hill of the long stone.
Bryn Mawr –	big hill.
Bryn Rhudd –	red hill.
Bwlch-gwyn –	white pass.
Caerfyrddin –	fort of Myrddin.
Cae'r Onnen –	field of the ash tree.
Cae'r Penrhos –	field of the head of the moorland.
Capel Dewi –	chapel of (St.) David.
Capel Gwynfe –	chapel of the blessed plain.
Capel Hendre –	chapel of the winter dwelling.
Capel Newydd –	new chapel.
Capel Seion –	Zion chapel.
Capel Tomos –	Thomas chapel.
Carn Wen –	white cairn.
Carreg Gwylan-fach –	stone of the little sea-gull.
Carreg Wastad –	flat stone.
Cas-blaidd –	wolf's fort or castle.
Cas-fuwch –	cow's fort or castle.
Casnewydd-bach –	little new fort.
Castellnewydd-Emlyn –	new castle in (the land of) Emlyn.
Castell Pictwn –	Picton's castle
Castell Rhingyll –	sergeant's castle.
Cef Carn-fadog –	ridge of Madog's cairn.
Cefneithin –	ridge of gorse.
Cefn Gwenffrwd –	ridge of the white stream.
Cefn Padrig –	Patrick's ridge.
Cef y Cnwc –	ridge of the hillock.
Cefn Ystrad-ffin –	ridge of the vale of the border.
Ceinewydd –	new quay.
Cilcennin –	source of the river Cennin.
Ciliau Aeron –	nooks of the river Aeron.
Cilrhedyn –	nook of fern.

Cil-sant – nook of a saint

Cil-y-cwm – retreat of the valley.

Clarach – flat land.

Clunderwen – meadow of an oak tree.

Cnwch-coch – red hillock.

Cynycau hillocks.

Coedwig Frechfa – forest of the mottled place.

Coed-y-bryn – wood of the hill.

Comins-coch – red common land.

Cors Goch
Glanteifi – red fen on the bank of the river Teifi.

Craig Fron-goch – rock of the red slope.

Cribyn – a crest.

Croes-goch – red cross.

Croesyceiliog – cross of the cockerel.

Crug Mawr – large cairn.

Crug Siarl – cairn of Charles.

Crug y Gorllwyn – cairn of the ambush.

Crwbin – a mound.

Crymych – where the oxen shiver or cower.

Cwmaman – valley of the river Aman.

Cwm-bach – little valley.

Cwmbrwyn – valley of rushes.

Cwm-du – black valley.

Cwmduad – valley of the river Duad.

Cwmfelinmynach – valley of the monk's mill.

Cwm-ffrwd – valley of the stream.

Cwmgwili – valley of the river Gwili.

Cwmifor – Ivor's valley.

Cwm-morgan – Morgan's valley.

Cwm-pen-graig – valley of the head of the rock.

Cwmsychbant – valley of the dry hollow.

Cwm-y-glo – valley of the coal.

Cwmystwyth – valley of the river Ystwyth (flexible).

Cwrt-henri – Henry's court.

Cwrtnewydd – new court.

Cwrtycadno – the fox's court.

Cynghordy – meeting house.

Derwen-gam – crooked oak tree.

Dibyn Du – black precipice.

Dinas – fort.

Dinbych-y-pysgod – small fort of the fish (of the sea).

Dolau Cothi – meadows of the river Cothi.

Dre-fach – little homestead.

Dryslwyn – thornbush.

Dyffryn – valley.

Dyffryn Llyfnant –	valley of the smooth-flowing stream.
Dyffryn Tywi –	valley of the river Tywi.
Efail-wen –	white smithy.
Eglwys-fach –	little church.
Eglwys-wythwr –	church of the eight men (or ministers).
Esgairdawe –	ridge of the river Tawe.
Esgair Hirnant –	ridge of the long stream.
Fedwen Fawr –	large birch tree.
Felindre –	homestead of the mill.
Felin-fach –	little mill.
Felin-gwm-isaf –	mill of the lower valley.
Felin-gwm-uchaf –	mill of the upper valley.
Felin-wen –	white mill.
Foel Cwmcerwyn –	bare hill of the valley of Cerwyn.
Foel Drygarn –	bare hill of the three cairns.
Foel Eryr –	bare hill of an eagle.
Foel Feddau –	bare hill of graves.
Foel Goch –	bare, red hill.
Ffair Fach –	little fair.
Ffair Rhos –	fair of the moorland.
Ffaldybrenin –	the King's sheep-fold.
Ffos-y-ffin –	ditch of the border.
Garn Fawr –	large cairn.
Garn Gron –	round cairn.
Garreg Lâs –	blue or green stone.
Garth-penrhyncoch –	enclosure of the red promontory.
Gelli-aur –	golden grove.
Gelli-wen –	white or fair grove.
Glanaman –	bank of the river Aman.
Glandŵr –	bank of the water.
Glynteg –	fair glen.
Gors-goch –	red marsh.
Hendy-gwyn-ar-dâf –	old white house on the river Tâf.
Henllan –	old church.
Llanbadarn Fawr –	large church of St. Padarn.
Llanbadrig –	church of St. Patrick.
Llanbedr pont Steffan –	church of St. Peter of Stephen's bridge.
LLandeilo Fawr –	big church of St. Teilo.
Llanddeusant –	church of two saints.
Llanfadog –	church of Madog.
Llan-fair –	church of St. Mary.
Llan-fair Nant-gwyn –	church of St. Mary of the white stream.

Llanfihangel-ar-arth (Iorath) –	St. Michael's church of Iorath.
Llanfynydd –	church of the mountain.
Llanfyrnach –	church of St. Brynach.
Llangwm –	church of the valley.
Llan-non –	church of Non.
Llanpumsaint –	church of five saints.
Llan-saint –	church of saints.
Llansanffraid –	church of St. Bridget.
Llansteffan –	church of St. Stephen.
Llan-y-cefn –	church of the ridge.
Llechryd –	flat stone ford.
Llwyncelyn –	holly bush.
Llwynhendy –	bush of the old house.
Llys-y-frân –	court of the crow.
Maes-llyn –	meadow of the pond or lake.
Maes-y-bont –	meadow of the bridge.
Maesycrugiau –	meadow of the cairns.
Meinciau –	benches.
Moelfre –	bare hill.
Moel y Garn –	bare hill of the cairn.
Moel y Llyn –	bare hill of the lake.
Moel y Môr –	bare hill of the sea.
Mynachlog-ddu –	black monastery.
Mynydd y Betws –	mountain of the prayer house.
Mynyddgarreg –	mountain of the stone.
Mynydd y Llan –	mountain of the church or parish.
Mynydd Ysgubor –	mountain of the barn.
Nant-y-caws –	stream of the cheese.
Nant-y-fallen –	stream of the apple-tree.
Pant-gwyn –	white hollow.
Parc-llyn –	parkland of the lake or pond.
Penalun –	Alun's headland.
Penbryn –	top of the hill.
Pencader –	top of the seat or fort.
Pen Caer –	top of the fort.
Pencarreg –	top of the rock.
Pen Coed-y-foel –	the end of the bare hill wood.
Pen Creigiau'r Llan –	the end of the rocks of the church or parish.
Penfro –	end of the country.
Pen-ffordd –	end of the road.
Penllechwen –	top of the white slate.
Pen Llwyn-uchel –	end of the high grove.
Penmaendewi –	head of David's rock.

Pennant – head of a valley or stream.
Penparcau – head of the parklands.
Pen-rhiw – top of the hillside.
Penrhiwclochdy – top of the hillside of the belfry.
Penrhiw-llan – top of the hillside of the church.
Pen Rhos – end of the moorland.
Penrhyn-coch – red promontory.
Pen-sarn – end of the paved way.
Pentre bach – little village.
Pentre-cwrt – village of the court.
Pentregalar – village of mourning
Pentre-isaf – lower village.
Pentre'r-felin – village of the mill.
Pentre-tŷ-gwyn – village of the white house.
Pentywyn – end of the shore.
Pen-y-banc – top of the bank.
Pen-y-bryn – top of the hill.
Pen y Bwlch – end of the pass.
Pen-y-cwm – head of the valley.
Pen-yr-allt – top of the hillside or wood.
Pen yr Hen Gastell – head of the old castle.
Pontaman – bridge over the river Aman.
Pontargothi – bridge over the river Cothi.
Ponterwyd – bridge of poles.
Pontgarreg – bridge of stone.
Pont-hirwaun – bridge of the long moorland.
Pont-rhyd-y-groes – bridge of the ford of the cross.
Pont-siân – Siân's bridge.
Porth-y-rhyd – gateway of the ford.
Pren-gwyn – white tree.
Pump-hewl – five roads.
Pumsaint – five saints.
Pwllcrochan – pool or pit of the cauldron.
Rhandir-mwyn – land of minerals.
Rhiw Cilgwyn – hill of the white recess or nook.
Rhos – moorland.
Rhosbwlch – moorland of the pass.
Rhosfarcut – moorland of the kite.
Rhos-maen – moorland of the stone.
Rhos-yr-hafod – moorland of the summer dwelling.
Rhydaman – ford of the river Aman.
Rhydcymerau – ford of the confluences.
Rhydfach – little ford.
Rhydlewis – ford of Lewis.

Rhydowen – ford of Owen.
Rhydypennau – ford of the hilltops.
Sancler – St. Clears.
Sant Ffraid – St. Bridget's (St. Bride's).
Sarnau – paved ways.
Swyddffynnon – region of the well or spring.
Tair Carn Uchaf – three higest cairns.
Talgarreg – front of the rock.
Tal-sarn – end of the paved way.
Tal-y-bont – end of the bridge.
Tan-y-bwlch – below the pass.

Tre-cŵn – homestead of dogs.
Treddraenen – homestead of the thornbush.
Trefdraeth – homestead of the beach.
Trefgarn – homestead of the cairn.
Trefgarnowen – homestead of Owen's cairn.
Treffynnon – homestead of the well.
Treherbert – Herbert's homestead.
Tre-lech – homestead of the slate.
Trelewelyn – homestead of Llewelyn.
Trewilym Ddwyreiniol – the eastern homsetad of William.
Trewilym Orllewinol – the western homstead of William.
Trichrug – three mounds.
Trisant – three saints.
Tyddewi – house of St. David.
Tywyn Mawr – large shore.
Waun Fawr – large meadow.
Y Betws – the house of prayer.
Y Bont Faen – the stone bridge.
Y Bont Newydd – the new bridge.
Y Borth – the harbour
Y Cerrig – the stones.
Y Gamallt – winding hillside (road).
Y Goedwig – the forest.
Ynys-lâs – green or blue island.
Yr Allt – the hillside or wood.
Yr Eglwys Lwyd – the holy or grey church.
Yr Hendy – the old house.

IV PLACE NAMES IN GWENT

Abergwenffrwd – mouth of the white stream.
Abersychan – mouth of the river Sychan (dry place).
Abertyleri – mouth of the river Tyleri.
Allteuryn – golden hillside.
Bâl Mawr – big summit.
Bedwellte – place of the fast flowing stream.
Betws Newydd – new prayer house.
Blaenafon – source of a river.
Blaenau – head of the valleys.
Bontnewydd-ar-Wysg – new beidge on the river Usk.
Bryn Mawr – big hill.
Cadffrwd – brook of the battle.
Caerllion – fort of the legion.
Caer-went – fort of Gwent (a field or plain).
Capel – Coed-y-mynach – chapel of the monk's wood.
Cas-bach – little fort.
Cas-gwent – fort of Gwent (a field or plain).
Casnewydd-ar-Wysg – new fort on the river Usk.
Castell Gwyn – white castle.
Castell Meirch – castle of stallions.
Cefn Coch – red ridge.
Cefn Manmoel – ridge of the bare place.
Cefn Pyllauduon – ridge of the black pools or pits.
Clydach – a river flowing through a shaded place.
Coed-duon – black wood.
Coed-y-paun – wood of the peacock.
Coed yr Iarll – the Earl's wood.
Croesyceiliog – cross of the cockerel.
Croes-y-mwyalch – cross of the blackbird.
Crugiau-forgan – Morgan's cairns.
Crymlyn – rounded glen.
Cwm – valley.
Cwmbrân – valley of the river Brân (crow).
Cwm-carn – valley of the cairn.
Cwmfelin-fach – valley of the little mill.
Cwmtyleri – valley of the river Tyleri.
Cwmynys y coed – valley of the island of wood.
Chwarel y fan – quarry of the peak.
Drenwydd Gelli-farch – new town of the stallion's grove.
Dyffryn – valley.
Eglwys y Drindod – the Trinity Church.

Felin-fach — little mill.
Felin-newydd — new mill.
Garndiffaith — desolate cairn or mound.
Garn-lydan — wide cairn.
Gellifelen — yellow grove.
Gilfach-fargod — little nook of the border.
Gilwern — nook or retreat of the marsh.
Glandŵr — bank of the water.
Glynebwy — valley of the river Ebwy.
Hafodyrynys — summer dwelling of the island.
Henllys — old court.
Is-coed — below the wood.
Llan-bedr — St. Peter's Church
Llandeilo Bertholau — St. Teilo's church of the fair copse.
Llanddewi nant Hodni — St. David's church of the Hodni stream.
Llanelen — church of St. Elen.
Llanfair Isgoed — St. Mary's church below the wood.
Llanfihangel Troddi — St. Michael's church of the Troddi river.
Llanfihangel-y-fedw — St. Michael's church of the birch trees.
Llan-ffwyst — church of St. Ffwyst.
Llangwm — church in the valley.
Llangybi — church of St. Cybi.
Llanhiledd — church of St. Hiledd.
Llanisien — church of St. Isan.
Llanmelin — church of the mill.
Llantrisaint — church of the three saints.
Llan-wern — church of the marsh.
Llwyncelyn — holly bush.
Maes-glas — green field.
Magwyr — enclosures.
Man-moel — bare place.
Mynydd-bach — little mountain.
Mynydd Carn-y-cefn — mountain of the cairn of the ridge.
Mynydd Carn-y-clochdy — mountain of the belfry cairn.
Mynyddislwyn — Islwyn's mountain.
Mynydd Maen — mountain of stone.
Mynydd Pen-y-fâl — top of Mountain (Sugar Loaf).
Mynydd y Gadair — mountain of the chair.
Mynydd y Grug — mountain of the heather.

Mynydd y Llan – mountain of the church or parish.
Nant-y-bwch – stream of the buck.
Nant-y-glo – stream of the coal.
Pandy – fulling mill.
Pant-teg – fair hollow.
Pen-allt – top of a slope.
Pengam – crooked top.
Penperllenni – top of the orchards.
Pentrepoeth – warm village.
Pen-twyn – top of the hill.
Pen-y-fan – top of the peak.
Pont-ap-hywel – bridge of Hywel's son.
Pont-hir – long bridge.
Pontnewydd – new bridge.
Pont-rhyd-yr-ynn – bridge of the ford of the ash trees.
Pont-y-moel – bridge of the bare hill.
Pont-y-pŵl Pontypool.
Pont-y-waun – bridge of the meadow or moor.
Pwll-gelen – pool of the leech.
Rhiwderyn – bird's hill.
Rhyd-y-meirch – ford of the stallions.
Tafarnau Bach – little taverns.
Tonypistyll – grassy plot of the spring or well.
Tredegar – homestead of Tegyr.
Trefonnen – homestead of the ash tree.
Treowen – Owen's homestead.
Tre'r-gaer – homestead of the fort.
Treruffudd – homestead of Gruffudd.
Tryleg – homestead of slate.
Tŷ-du – black house.
Waun-lwyd – grey meadow or moorland.
Y Betws – the house of prayer.
Y Gwastad – the plain.
Y Maendy – the stone house.
Y Maerdy – the dairy house or steward's house.
Ynys Ddu – black island.
Yr Eglwys Newydd ar y cefn – the new church on the ridge.
Yr Hengastell – the old castle.
Yr Isga – the lower field.

V PLACE NAMES IN GWYNEDD

Aberangell – mouth of the river Angell (wing or tributory).
Abercegin – mouth of the river Cegin.
Abercywarch – mouth of the river Cywarch (hemp).
Aberdaron – mouth of the river Daron.
Aberdyfi – mouth of the river Dyfi.
Aber-erch – mouth of the river Erch (mottled).
Aberffro – mouth of the river Ffraw.
Aberglaslyn – mouth of the river Glaslyn (blue or silver lake).
Aberllefenni – mouth of the river Llefenni (elm trees).
Abermawddach – mouth of the river Mawddach.
Abersoch – mouth of the river Soch.
Amlwch – land bordering a lake.
Beddgelert – the grave of Gelert.
Bera Mawr – large stock.
Betws Garmon – prayer house of Garmon.
Betws-y-coed – prayer house in the wood.
Blaenau Ffestiniog – the heads of the valleys in the land of Ffestin.
Bont-ddu – black bridge.
Bontnewydd – new bridge.
Brithdir – mottled land.
Bron-y-foel – bare hillside.
Bryn-crug – the hill of the cairn.
Bryn-mawr – big hill.
Bryn'refail – hill of the smithy.
Brynsiencyn – hill of Siencyn.
Bryn-teg – fair hill.
Bwlch Mawr – large pass.
Bwlch y Ddeufaen – the pass of the two stones.
Bwlch y Gwyddyl – the pass of the Irish.
Cadair Idris – the chair of Idris.
Caernarfon – fort in Arfon.
Capel Coch – red chapel.
Capel Curig – the chapel of (St.) Curig.
Capel Gwyn – white chapel.
Capel Mawr – big chapel.
Carnedd Ddafydd – cairn of David.
Carnedd Llywelyn – cairn of (Prince) Llywelyn.
Carreg Ddu – black stone.
Carreg-lefn – smooth stone.
Carreg-y-saeth – the stone of the arrow.
Castell Penrhyn – castle of the promontory .

Castell Tomen-y-mur –	castle of the mound of the wall.
Cefn Caer Euni (Cefn Creini) –	the ridge of the fort of Euni.
Cefn Du –	black ridge.
Coed y Brenin –	wood of the king.
Corlan Fraith –	speckled pen or fold.
Cors Geirch –	fen of oats.
Craig Cwmllwyd –	the rock of the holy or grey-brown valley.
Craig Dôl-fudr –	the rock of the dirty meadow.
Craig y Llyn –	the rock of the lake.
Cutiau –	huts or cottages.
Cwm Cewydd –	valley of Cewydd.
Cwm Hirnant –	valley of the long stream.
Cwm-y-glo –	valley of coal.
Diffwys –	steep slope or wilderness.
Dinas –	a camp or fort.
Dinas Mawr –	large camp or fort.
Dolbenmaen –	meadow at the head of a rock.
Dolgellau –	meadow of (monk's) cells.
Efailnewydd –	new smithy.
Eglwys-bach –	small church.
Esgair Berfa –	mountain ridge of the wheelbarrow .
Foel Boeth –	warm, bare hill.
Foel Ddu –	black, bare hill.
Foel Ganol –	middle, bare hill.
Foel Goch –	red, bare hill.
Foel Offrwm –	bare hill of sacrifice.
Foel Wen –	white, bare hill.
Foel y Geifr –	bare hill of the goats.
Foel yr Hydd –	bare hill of the stag.
Fron-goch –	red hillside.
Garn Boduan –	cairn of Boduan.
Garndolbenmaen –	cairn of the meadow at the head of a rock.
Garnedd Goch –	red cairn.
Gellilydan –	wide grove.
Glan-aber –	bank of the estuary.
Glan-rhyd –	bank of the ford.
Glanyrafon –	bank of the river.
Glan y Wern –	bank of the marsh.
Glyn –	glen.
Graig Goch –	red rock.
Graig Wen –	white rock.
Gwastadros –	flat moorland.

Harlech – beautiful slate.
Heneglwys – old church.
Henryd – old ford.
Llain-goch – red blade.
Llanaber – church of the river mouth.
Llanbedr – church of St. Peter.
Llanbedrycennin – St. Peter's church of the leeks.
Llandudno – church of St, Tudno.
Llanddeusant – church of two saints.
Llanfair – church of St. Mary.
Llanfair-is-gaer – church of St, Mary below the fort.
Llanfair-pwll-gwyngyll-gogerychwyrndrobwll-llantysilio-gogogoch – St. Mary's church – in a hollow – white hazels – near to the rapid whirlpool – St. Tysil's church – red cave.
Llanfair-yn-y-Cwmwd – St. Mary's church in the commote.
Llanfihangel-y-traethau – St. Mary's church of the beaches.
Llan Ffestiniog – church of the land of Ffestin.
Llangoed – church of the wood.
Llannerch-y-Medd – glade of the mead.
Llan-rhos – church of the moorland.
Llansanffraid Glan Conwy – St. Bridget's church on the bank of the Conway. Conway.
Llanuwchllyn – church above the lake.
Llanycil – church of the retreat.
Llidiardau – gates.
Llwyndyrys – tangled grove.
Maen Addwyn – fine rock.
Maen-y-Bugail – rock of the shepherd.
Mallwyd – grey field.
Marian-glas – blue moraine.
Melin-y-coed – mill of the wood.
Minffordd – edge of the road.
Minllyn – edge of the lake or pool.
Moel Ddu – black, bare hill.
Moelfre – bare hill.
Moel Llechwedd Hafod – bare hill of the slope of the summer dwelling.
Moel Llyfnant – bare hill of the smooth stream.
Moel Meirch – bare hill of the horses.

Moel Oernant – bare hill of the cold stream.
Moel y Cerrigduon – bare hill of the black stones.
Moel y Llechau – bare hill of the slates.
Moel Ymenyn – bare hill of butter.
Moel yr Hydd – bare hill of the stag.
Moel Ysgyfarnogod – bare hill of the hares
Morfa Bychan – little fen.
Morfa Gwyllt – wild fen.
Morfa Harlech – fen of the beautiful slate.
Mynydd Craig-goch – red-rock mountain.
Mynydd Cwm-mynach – monk's valley mountain.
Mynydd Drws-y-coed – door-of-the-wood mountain.
Mynydd Pencoed – end of the wood mountain.
Mynydd Pennant – head of the valley mountain.
Mynydd Tirycwmwd – the mountain of the commote land.

Mynydd Tŵr – tower mountain.
Nant-y-pandy – stream of the fulling mill.
Nasareth – biblical name – Nazareth.
Pandy – fulling mill.
Pant Glas – green valley or hollow.
Pencaenewydd – head of the new field.
Penffridd-sarn – head of the paved sheep walk.
Penisa'r-waun – lower end of the meadow.
Penllech – end of the slate. (Anglesey – Benllech).
Penllithrig-y-wrach – slippery head of the witch.
Penmaen-mawr – end of the large stone.
Penmorfa – end of the fen.
Penmynydd – head of the mountain.
Pennant – head of the strean or valley.
Penrhos – end of the moorland.
Penrhyn – promontory.
Penrhyndeudraeth – promontory of two beaches.
Pen-sarn – end of the paved way.
Pentir – headland.
Pentraeth – end of the beach.
Pentre-bont – village of the bridge.
Pentre'r-felin – village of the mill.
Pentre Tafarnyfedw – village of the birch trees tavern.

Pen-y-ffridd – head of the sheep walk.
Pen-y-garn – head of the cairn.
Pistyll – spring or well.
Pont Penybenglog – bridge of the skull.
Pont-y-pant – bridge of the hollow.
Pren-teg – fair wood.
Pwll-defaid – sheep's pool or pit.
Pwllheli – pool of salt water.
Pydew – well or pit.
Rhaeadr Ewynnol – foaming waterfall.
Rhiwlas – green hillside or slope.
Rhobell Fawr – large saddle-like ridge.
Rhos-fawr – large moorland.
Rhos-goch – red moorland.
Rhos-hir – long moorland.
Rhos-meirch – moorland of the horses.
Rhos-y-llan – moorland of the church or parish.
Rhyd – ford.
Rhyd-ddu – black ford.
Rhyd-wyn – white ford.
Rhydyclafdy – ford of the hospital.
Rhydygwystl – ford of the pledge or hostage.
Sarn – paved roadway.
Sarnau – end of the paved ways.
Talwrn – rocky place.
Tal-y-bont – end of the bridge.
Tal-y-llyn – end of the lake.
Tal-y-sarn – end of the paved way.
Tan-y-graig – below the rock.
Tanygrisau – below the steps.
Tan-yr-allt – below the wood or hillside.
Traeth Bach – little beach.
Trawsfynydd – across the mountain.
Trefdraeth – homestead of the beach.
Trefgraig – homestead of the rock.
Trefor – homestead of the sea.
Treffynnon – homestead of the well.
Tre-garth – homestead of the ridge or enclosure.
Trum Gelli – crest of the grove.
Trwyn Maen Dylan – promontory of Dylan's rock.
Trwyn y Fuwch – promontory or nose of the cow.
Trwyn y Mynydd – promontory of the mountain.
Twll Du – black hole.
Tŷ-hen – old house.
Tyn-y-pwll – small holding of the pool.
Uwchmynydd – above the mountain.

Waunfawr –	large meadow.
Waun Oer –	cold meadow.
Waun y Griafolen –	meadow of mountain ash.
Y Bala –	where a river flows from a lake.
Y Drum –	the summit.
Y Dduallt –	the black wood or hillside.
Y Rhiw –	the hill.
Ysbyty Ifan –	hospital of Ifan (Evan).

VI PLACE NAMES IN (MID)–GLAMORGAN

Abaty Margam –	the abbey of Morgan (the Courteous or Morgan ab Caradog).
Aberbargod –	mouth of river Bargod (boundary).
Abercannaid –	where the rivulet Cannaid (white) flows into the river Taf.
Aberdâr –	mouth of the river Dâr (oak trees).
Aberfan –	where the Fan (high) stream flows into the river Taf.
Aber-nant –	mouth of the stream.
Aberogwr –	mouth of the river Ogwr.
Abertridwr –	confluence of three brooks.
Bargod –	boundary or march.
Bedlinog –	either a grove of birch trees or the grave of a fox.
Beddau –	graves.
Betws –	House of prayer.
Blaen-cwm –	end of the valley.
Blaengarw –	source of the river Garw (coarse or rough).
Blaenllechau –	source of the river Hechau (rocky).
Blaenrhondda –	source of the river Rhondda (black hue).
Bryncethin –	dark or frightful hill.
Bryngolau –	light or fair hill.
Brynmenyn –	hill of butter or stony hill.
Brynsadler –	hill of the sadler.
Bryn-y-cae –	hill of the field.
Cadair Fawr –	large chair or seat.
Caerau –	enclosed forts.
Caerffili –	fort of Philip or Ffili.
Carn y Bugail –	cairn of the shepherd.
Cefncoedycymer –	woody ridge of the confluence.
Cefn gelli-gaer –	ridge of the grove of the fort.
Cefn glas –	green ridge.

Cefn Hirgoed –	ridge of the long wood.
Cefn Merthyr –	ridge of the martyr.
Cefnpennar –	ridge of the end of the arable land.
Cefn Pyllauduon –	ridge of the black pools or pits.
Cefn y Rhondda –	ridge of the Rhondda (black hue).
Cilfynydd –	a mountain recess.
Clwydyfagwyr –	gate of the wall.
Coedwig Sain Gwynno –	St. Gwynno's Forest.
Coety –	a wood-house or a house in the wood.
Craig yr efail –	rock of the smithy.
Creigiau –	rocks.
Cwmaman –	valley of the river Aman.
Cwm-bach –	small valley.
Cwmclydach –	valley of the river Clydach (river which flows through a sheltered place).
Cwmdâr –	valley of the river Dâr (oak trees).
Cwmfelin –	valley of the mill.
Cwm-Ogwr –	valley of the river Ogwr.
Cwm-parc –	valley of parkland.
Cynffig –	a corruption of Cefn-y-Figen = the ridge above the fen.
Deri –	oak trees.
Dinas –	fort or camp.
Dinas isaf –	lower fort or camp.
Drenewydd –	new town.
Dyffryn –	valley.
Efailisaf –	lower smithy.
Ewenni –	the frothy water.
Fochriw –	hillside of the pigs.
Ffynnon Taf –	Taf's well.
Gelli-gaer –	grove of the fort.
Gilfach-goch –	red retreat.
Glan-bad –	bank or shore of the boat.
Glan-llyn –	shore of the pool or lake.
Glyn-coch –	red glen.
Glyn-taf –	glen of the river Taf.
Gwaelod-y-garth –	base of the ridge.
Gwaun caerffili –	meadow or moor of the fort of Philip or Ffili.
Hirwaun –	long meadow.
Llangynwyd –	church of St. Cynwyd.
Llanharan –	church dedicated to Aaron.
Llanhari –	church of Garai.
Llanilltyd Faerdref –	Church of St. Illtyd near the dairy house.
Llantrisant –	church of three saints.

Llanwynno –	church of Gwynno.
Llechryd –	slate ford.
Llwyn-onn –	ash grove.
Llwynypia –	bush of the magpie.
Maesteg –	fair field.
Maesycymer –	field of the river confluence.
Meisgyn –	the lord or leader's land.
Melin Ifan Ddu –	the mill of Evan the Black.
Merthyr Tudful –	Tudful, the martyr. (Tudful = the murdered daughter of Brychan Brycheiniog).
Mynwent y crynwyr –	Quaker's graveyard (yard).
Mynydd Aberdâr –	mountain of the mouth of the river Dâr (oak trees).
Mynydd bach –	little mountain.
Mynydd cynffig –	mountain ridge above the fen. (Kenfig Hill).
Mynydd Eglwysilan –	mountain of the church of Elian or Elen.
Mynydd Fochriw –	the mountain of the pigs' slope.
Mynydd Merthyr –	the mountain of the martyr.
Mynydd Tynewydd –	the mountain of the new house.
Mynydd y Gaer –	the mountain of the fort.
Mynydd y Glyn –	the mountain of the glen.
Mynydd y Gwair –	the mountain of the hay.
Nantgarw –	rough brook.
Nant-y-moel –	stream of the bare hill.
Pantysgallog –	a hollow full of thistles.
Pen-coed –	top of the wood.
Penpedairheol –	end of four roads.
Penrhiwceibr –	a corruption of Pen-Rhiw-Cae-Byr – top of the hillside in the small field.
Pentre-bach –	little village.
Pentre Ifan –	Evan's village.
Pentre-rhondda –	village of the river Rhondda (black hue).
Pen-twyn –	top of the mound.
Pen-tyrch –	headland of the ox.
Pent-y-bont ar Ogwr –	end of the bridge on the river Ogwr.
Penydarren –	top of a rocky hill.
Pen-y-fai –	end of the plain.
Pen-y-foel –	top of the bare hill.
Pen-y-graig –	top of the rock.
Penyrheol –	end of the road.
Penyrheolgerrig –	end of the stone road.

Pen-y-waun – end of the meadow or moor.
Pontbrenllwyd – grey wooden bridge or holy wooden bridge.
Pont-rhyd-y-cyff – bridge of the ford of the tree trunks.
Pontsticill – the bridge of the stile.
Pont-y-clun – bridge of the meadow.
Pontycymer – bridge of the confluence.
Pont-y-gwaith – bridge of the works (ironworks).
Pontypridd – from Pont-y-tŷ-pridd – bridge of the earthen house.
Porth-cawl – possibly, port of the Gauls.
Rhydri – slope of the oak trees.
Rhydyfelin – the ford of the mill.
Sarn – a paved way.
Senghennydd – St. Cenydd.
Tir-phil – land of Philip.
Ton-du – from Ton-ithel-Ddu – the grassy patch of land of Ithel the Black.
Ton-pentre – grassy plot at the end of the homestead.
Ton-teg – fair, grassy plot.
Tonypandy – grassy plot of the fulling mill.
Tonyrefail – the smithy on a grassy plot.
Tonysguboriau – barns on a grassy plot.
Traeth cynffig – the beach of the ridge above the fen.
Trealaw – the homestead of Alaw Goch (Alaw the Red).
Trebanog – the high homestead.
Tredomos – the homestead of Thomas.
Trefforest – homestead near the forest.
Tregynon – homestead of Cynon.
Trehafod – homestead of the summer dwelling.
Treharris – Harris' town.
Treherbert – a homestead named in honour of Herbert (of the Bute family).
Trelewis – Lewis' town.
Troed-y-rhiw – bottom or foot of the hill.
Twyn-y-waun – mound of the meadow.
Tynewydd – new house.
Tyn-y-bryn – small holding of the hill.
Tyn-y-coedcae – small holding of the wood field.
Tywyn cynffig – sea shore of the ridge above the fen.
Y Garth – the enclosure.
Y Goetre hen – the old homstead in the wood.
Y Groes-faen – the stone cross.
Y Groes-wen – the white cross.
Y Maerdy – the dairy house.
Ynys-hir – long island.
Ynysowen – Owen's island.

Ynys-y-bŵl –	the island of the pit or ball.
Y Pîl –	the creek.
Y Porth –	the gateway.
Y Rugos –	the place of heather.
Ystradmynach –	valley of the monk.
Ystradyfodwg –	the valley of St. Tyfodwg.
Y Wig –	the wood.

VII PLACE NAMES IN (SOUTH) GLAMORGAN

Aberddawan –	mouth of the river Ddawan.
Aberthin –	place of sacrfices.
Caerau –	forts or camps.
Caerdydd –	fort on the Taf (Taf>Dyf>Dydd).
Cogan –	named after the Cogan family.
Cwm-elái –	valley of the Elái river.
Dinas Powis –	probably named after Denis, daughter of the Prince of Powys.
Eglwys Brewis –	church of Breos (probably named after Wm. de Breos, Bishop of Llandaf, 1265).
Eglwys Fair y Mynydd –	St. Mary's Church on the mountain.
Ffontygari –	Ceri's well.
Gwénfo –	white or sacred place.
Lecwydd –	corruption of Llechwedd – a slope.
Llandbedr-y-fro –	St. Peter's church in the Vale (of Glamorgan). (**Peterston-super-Ely**).
Llancarfan –	church of St. Carfan.
Llancatal –	corruption of Llancadle – church on the battlefield.
Llandaf –	church of the river Taf.
Llandochwy –	church of St. Dochwy.
Llanddunwyd –	church of St. Dunwyd.
Llanedern –	church of Ederyn.
Llan-faes –	church of the field.
Llanfair –	St. Mary's church.
Llanfihangel-ar-Elái –	St. Michael's church on the river Elái
Llanfihangel y Bont-faen –	St. Michael's church of the stone bridge.
Llanfihangel-y-pwll –	St. Michael's church of the pool or pit.
Llanfleiddan –	church of Bleiddian.
Llanilltud fawr –	the greater church of St. Illtyd.

Llanisien –	church dedicated to Isan.
Llansanffraid-ar-Elái –	St. Bridget:s church on the river Elái.
Llantriddyd –	church of Treiddyd.
Llys-faen –	stone court.
Llyswyrny –	corruption of Llys-bro-nudd – the court of thr region of St, Nudd.
Marcroes –	the cross of St. Mark.
Merthyr Dyfan –	Dyfan the martyr (first bishop of Llandaf).
Penarth –	end of the promontory.
Penarth isaf –	lower end of the promontory.
Pendeulwyn –	top of the two groves.
Pen-llin –	end of the lake.
Pentremeurig –	village of Meurig.
Pentre-poeth –	warm village or dry village.
Pen-twyn –	top of the hill.
Porth-ceri –	port of Ceri (Ceri ab Caid).
Radur –	cheap or free land.
Sain Dunwyd –	St. Dunwyd.
Sain Ffagan –	St. Fagan.
Sain Nicolas –	St. Nicholas.
Sain Siorys –	St. George.
Sain Andras –	St. Andrew.
Sain Tathan –	St. Tathan.
Sili –	from Abersili, the mouth of the rivulet Sili (hissing water).
Tongwynlais –	green-blue plot of land.
Tregolwyn –	Colwyn's town or homestead.
Trelái –	homestead on the river Elái.
Tremorfa –	homestead of the sea-marsh.
Tresimwn –	Simon's homstead.
Trwyn Larnog –	the point of Llanwernog (church in a meadow).
Y Barri –	either 'the limit of the water' or a reference to the de Barry family.
Y Bont-faen –	the stone bridge.
Y Maendy –	the stone house.
Ynys Sili –	the island of the rivulet Sili.
Ynys y Barri –	Barry island (see Y Barri).
Y Rhis –	the moorland.
Yr Eglwys Newydd –	the new church.
Ystradowen –	Owen's valley.

VIII PLACE NAMES IN (WEST) GLAMORGAN

Aberafan –	mouth of the river Afan.
Aberdulais –	junction of the rivers Dulais and Nedd.
Abergwynfi –	mouth of the Gwynfi stream.
Abertawe –	mouth of the river Tawe (quiet river).
Allt y grug –	hill or wood of the heather.
Bae Abertawe –	the boy of the mouth of the Tawe river.
Baglan –	from Llanfaglan – church of St. Baglan.
Blaendulais –	source of the Dulais river.
Blaengwynfi –	source of the Gwynfi river.
Bryn –	hill.
Brynaman-isaf –	the lower hill of the Aman river.
Bryn-coch –	red hill.
Bryn mawr –	big hill.
Bwlchmynydd –	the mountain pass.
Casllwchwr –	from Castell Llwchwr – the castle of the inlet of water.
Castell-nedd –	the castle on the river Nedd.
Cefn Bryn –	ridge of the hill.
Cefn morfudd –	Morfudd's ridge.
Cilá –	from Cilfai – a retreat on the plain.
Cilâ uchaf –	the upper retreat on the plain.
Cil-ffriw –	retreat on the hilltop.
Cilmaen-gwyn –	white stone retreat.
Cilybebyll –	retreat of the tents.
Clydach –	a river flowing throuhg a shaded place.
Craig-cefn-parc –	the rock of the ridge in a field.
Craig y Llyn –	rock of the lake or pond.
Cwm –	valley.
Cwmafan –	valley of the river Afan.
Cwm-gwrach –	valley of the witch.
Cwmllynfell –	corruption of Llyfnell – valley of the smooth-flowing river.
Cwmrhydyceirw –	valley of the stags' ford.
Cwm Tawe –	valley of the river Tawe.
Drenewydd –	new town.
Dyffryn –	valley.
Dynfant –	corruption of Dwfnant – deep stream.
Efail-fach –	little smithy.
Faerdre –	homestead of the dairy.
Felindre –	homstead of the mill.
Fforest fach –	little forest.
Garn-swllt –	cairn of treasure.
Gelli-nudd –	misty grove.
Glandŵr –	bank of the water.
Glyncorrwg –	glen of the two corrwg streams.

Glyn-nedd – glen of the Nedd river.
Godre'r graig – foot of the rock.
Gorseinon – the fen of Einion.
Graig fawr – large rock.
Heol-lâs – blue or green road.
Hirfynydd – long mountain.
Llandeilo Ferwallt – church of Bishop Teilo.
Berwallt – Berw (water cress) allt-(wooded slope).
Llanddewi – church of St. David.
Llangatwg – church of St. Catwg.
Llangyfelach – church of Cyfelach (bishop of Llandaf).
Llangynydd – church of Cenydd.
Llanilltud Gŵyr – church of St. Illtud in Gower.
Llanmadog – church of Madog.
Llanrhidian – church of Rhidian.
Llansamlet – church of Samled.
Llan-y-tair-mair – church of the three Marys.
Maes Awyr Abertawe – Swansea Airport.
Margam – from the personal name Morgan.
Melin-cwrt – mill of the court.
Moel ton-mawr – bare hill of the large grassy plot.
Moel yr Hyrddod – bare hill of the rams.
Morfa Llanrhidian – sea marsh of the church of Rhidian.
Mynydd Caerau – mountain of forts.
Mynydd Dinas – mountain of the camp or fort.
Mynydd Margam – Morgan's mouutain.
Mynydd Pen-hydd – stag's head mountain.
Myndyd Pen-cae – top-of-the-field mountain.
Mynydd Pysgodlyn – fish-pond mountain.
Mynydd Uchaf – highest mountain.
Mynydd y Garn fach – mountain of the little cairn.
Mynydd y Garth – mountain of the enclosure.
Pen-clawdd – end of the embankment.
Pengelli – end of the grove.
Penlle'r gaer – top of the fortress.
Pen-maen – head of the stone.
Pennard – top of the hill.
Pen Pwll-du – head of the black pool.
Penrhiw-fawr – top of the long hillside.

Penrhyn Gŵyr –	the promontory of the curving land (Gower).
Pen-rhys –	the head of Rhys ab Caradog (beheaded by the Normans).
Pentreclwyda –	village of gates.
Pentre-dŵr –	village of water.
Pentwyn mawr –	top of the large mound.
Pen-y-fai –	end of the plain.
Penyrheol –	end of the road.
Pontardawe –	bridge on the river Tawe (quiet).
Pontarddulais –	bridge on the river Dulais (dark blue).
Pont-lliw –	bridge on the river Lliw (lake or hollow).
Pont-rhyd-y-fen –	bridge on the ford of the river Afan.
Pontwalby –	Walby's bridge.
Porth Talbot –	a harbour named after the Talbot family.
Porth Tennant –	a harbour built by H. T. Tennant of Cadoxton Lodge.
Porth Einon –	the port of Einion.
Pwll-y-glaw –	the rain pool.
Resolfen –	a gazing place.
Rhos Margam –	Morgan's moorland.
Rhos-sili –	moorland of the sea.
Rhyd-y-fro –	ford or stream of the vale.
Sgiwen –	from Is-cae-ywen – below the field of the yew tree.
Tai-bach –	small houses.
Tai'r gwaith –	houses of the works.
Tai'r-ysgol –	school houses.
Ton-mawr –	large grassy plot.
Tonna –	grassy plots of land.
Traeth Aberafan –	the beach of the mouth of the river Afan.
Traeth Abertawe –	the beach of the mouth of the river Tawe.
Traeth Llandrhidian –	the beach of the church of Rhidian.
Traeth Margam –	Morgan's beach.
Traeth Rhos-sili –	the sands of the moor of the sea.
Trebannws –	homestead of the hilltops.
Treforys –	the homestead of Morris (Sir John Morris, founder of the copper works round which the town grew).
Tre-gŵyr –	the homestead of Gower (curving land).
Trwyn porth einion –	the point of Einion's port.
Tynewydd –	new house.
Waunarlwydd –	lord's meadow.

Y Clun –	the meadow.
Y Creunant –	the narrow or clear stream.
Y Crwys –	corruption of Y Croes – the cross.
Y Cymer –	the confluence.
Y Goetre –	the homstead of wood, or in the wood.
Y Groes –	the cross or crossroads.
Ynysforgan –	Morgan's island.
Ynystawe –	the island of the river Tawe.
Yr Allt Wen –	the white wooded slope.
Ystalyfera –	the hay stall.
Ystumllwynarth –	shape or form of the buttress on the hill.

IX PLACE NAMES IN POWYS

Abercegyr –	mouth of the river Cegyr (hem lock).
Aberclydach –	mouth of the river Clydach (shaded place).
Abercraf –	mouth of the river Craf (garlic).
Aberedw –	mouth of the river Edw.
Abergwesyn –	mouth of the river Gwesyn.
Aberhonddu –	mouth of the river Honddu.
Aberhosan –	mouth of the river Rhosan (river of the moor).
Aberllynfi –	mouth of the river Llynfi (smooth).
Aber-miwl –	mouth of the river Miwl.
Aberriw –	mouth of the river Rhiw (hillside river).
Abertridwr –	confluence of three waters.
Abertwymyn –	mouth of the river Twymyn (warm or feverish water).
Allt Ddu –	black hillside.
Allt Goch –	red hillside.
Allt Lwyd –	brown or grey hillside.
Allt y Gadair –	hillside of the chair.
Allt yr Eryr –	wood of the eagle.
Banc y Celyn –	the holly bank.
Betws Cedewain –	the prayer house of Cedewain.
Blaengwy –	source of the river Wye.
Bron Felen –	yellow hillside.
Bronllys –	court of rushes.
Bryn Amlwg –	a clearly-seen hill.
Bryn Bach –	little hill.
Bryn Beili –	hill of the enclosure.
Bryn Bugeilaid –	hill of shepherds.

Bryn Camlo – hill of the river Camlo.
Bryn Coch – red hill.
Bryn Crugog – hill of the cairn.
Bryn Crwn – round hill.
Bryn Du – black hill.
Bryn Eithinog – hill of gorse.
Bryn Garw – rough or rocky hill.
Bryn Glâs – green hill.
Bryn Glasgwm – hill of the green valley.
Bryn Gwyn – white hill.
Bryn Llanbedr – the hill of St. Peter's church.
Bryn Llandeilo – the hill of St. Teilo's church.
Bryn Llanwen – hill of the white church.
Bryn Mawr – big hill.
Bryn y Begwn – hill of the beacon.
Bryn y Castell – castle hill.
Bryn y Gadair – hill of the chair.
Bryn y Maen – hill of the stone.
Bryn yr Oerfa – hill of the col place.
Bugeildy – house of the shepherd.
Bugeilyn – pasture of the shepherd.
Bwlch – a pass.
Bwlch y Ffridd – the sheep-walk pass.
Bwlch-y-Sarnau – pass of the paved roadways.
Caehopcyn – the field of Hopcyn.
Cae'r-lan – field of the river bank.
Camlas Mynwy a Brycheiniog – the Monmouthshire and Brecon Canal.
Capel Dyffryn – Honddu – the chapel of the vally of the Honddu river.
Capel-y-ffin – chapel of the border.
Carneddau – cairns.
Carnedd Wen – white cairn.
Carn Gwilym – Gwilym's cairn.
Carno – a placeof cairns.
Carreg Bica – sharp rock.
Carreg Goch – red stone.
Carreg Lwyd – grey stone.
Castell Caereinion – the castle of Einion's fort.
Castell Coch – red castle.
Castell Dinas – castle of the fort or camp.
Castell Maen – stone castle.
Cefn Carnedd – ridge of the cairn.
Cefn Cenarth – ridge of lichen.
Cefn Coch – red ridge.
Cefn Crin – dry ridge.

Cefn Gläs –	green ridge.
Cefn Ridge –	ridge of heather.
Cefn Gwyntog –	windy ridge.
Cefn Hir –	long ridge.
Cefn-llys –	ridge of the court.
Cefn y Grug –	ridge of the heather.
Cefn yr Ystrad –	ridge of the valley.
Cegidfa –	place of the hemlock.
Cemais –	bend in the river.
Cilmeri –	retreat of brambles.
Clas-ar-wy –	cloister on the river Wye.
Cnwclas –	green hillock.
Coedwig y Clun –	forest of the meadow.
Coed y Gaer –	wood of the fort.
Coed yr Ynys –	wood of the island.
Comins Coch –	red commons.
Coron y Ffridd –	top of the mountain pasture.
Craig Cerrig-gleisiad –	rock of the young. salmon's stones.
Craig y Nos –	rock of the night.
Croes y Forwyn –	cross of the virgin.
Crucywel –	cairn of Hywel.
Crugion –	cairns.
Crug Mawr –	large cairn.
Crugyn Llwyd –	grey cairn.
Cwm-bach –	little valley.
Cwmbach Llechryd –	little valley of the slate ford.
Cwmbelan –	valley of the round hill.
Cwmgiedd –	valley of the river Giedd.
Cwm-hir –	long valley.
Cwm Pennant –	valley of the head of a stream.
Cwm-twrch –	valley of the river Twrch (a boar).
Cwrt y Gollen –	court of the hazel tree.
Darowen –	Owen's oak trees.
Derwen-gam –	crooked oak-tree.
Disgwylfa –	watching place.
Dolau –	meadows.
Dôl-fach –	little meadow.
Dolfor –	big meadow.
Drum yr Eira –	ridge of the snow.
Drysgol –	rough land.
Dyffryn Llyfnant –	valley of the smooth stream.
Dylife –	flood waters.
Esgair Ddafydd –	David's ridge.
Esgair Ddu –	black ridge.
Esgairgeiliog –	the ridge of the cockerel.

Esgair Pen-y-Garreg –	the ridge of the summit of the tone.
Esgair y Groes –	the ridge of the cross.
Fan Bwlch Chwyth –	peak of the windy pass.
Fan Hir –	long peak.
Fan Nedd –	peak of the river Nedd.
Felindre –	homestead of the mill.
Felin-fach –	little mill.
Felin Newydd –	new mill.
Foel Fawr –	big bare hill.
Fron –	a hillside.
Fforest Fach –	little forest.
Fforest Fawr –	large forest.
Ffrwd Grech –	rippling brook.
Garreg Fawr –	large stone.
Garth –	enclosure.
Gaufron –	enclosed hillside.
Geuffordd –	road in a hollow or dip.
Glan-rhyd –	bank of the ford.
Glasbwll –	blue or green pool.
Glasgwm –	green valley.
Glaslyn –	blue lake.
Gors Lydan –	wide marsh.
Groes-ffordd –	crossroads.
Groes-lwyd –	holy or grey cross.
Gwaun Nant-ddu –	meadow or moor of the black stream.
Gwenddwr –	white water.
Hen Domen –	old mound.
Hen Gerrig –	old stones.
Heolsenni –	road of the river Senni.
Hirnant –	long stream or valley.
Llan –	church or parish.
Llanbadarn Fynydd –	St. Padarn's church of the mountain;
Llanbadarn Garreg –	St. Padarn's church of the rocks.
Llanbedr Ystrad Yw –	St. Peter's church in the valley of yew trees.
Llanbryn-mair –	church of St. Mary on the hill.
Llandrindod –	church of the Trinity.
Llandysul –	church of St. Tysul.
Llanfadog –	church of Madog.
Llanfaes –	church in a meadow.
Llanfair Caereinion –	St. Mary's church of Einion's fort.

Llan Fawr – large church or parish.
Llanfihangel – St. Michael's church.
Llanfihangel Cwm Du – St. Michael's church of the black valley.
Llanfihangel Dyffryn Arwy – St. Michael's church of the Arwy valley.
Llanfinhangel Fechan – little church of St. Michael.
Llanfihangel Nant Brân – St. Michael's church on the Brân river.
Llanfihangel Rhydieithon – St. Michael's church on the ford of the river Ithon.
Llanfihangel Tal-y-llyn – St. Michael's church at the head of the lake.
Llanfrynach – church of St. Brynach.
Llangamarch – church on the river Camarch.
Llan-gors – church of the marshland.
Llangurig – church of St. Curig.
Llannewydd – new church.
Llansanffraid – St. Birdget's church.
Llan-y-wern – church of the marsh.
Llawr-y-glyn – floor of the glen.
Llechwedd Hirgoed – slope of the long wood.
Llechwedd Mawr – large slope.
Llys-wen – white court.
Machynlleth – the field of Cynllaith.
Maen Rhisiart – Richard's stone.
Meifod – half-way dwelling-house.
Melin-y-ddôl – mill of the meadow.
Moelfre – bare hill.
Moel Hywel – bare hill of Hywel.
Moel Sych – dry, bare hill.
Moel y Llyn – bare hill of the lake.
Mynachdy – monastery.
Mynydd Bach Trecastell – little mountain of the homstead of the castle.
Mynydd Bwlch y Groes – mountain of the pass of the cross.
Mynydd Cerrigllwydion – mountain of the grey stones.
Mynydd Coch – red mountain.
Mynydd Fforest – mountain of the forest.

Mynydd Llan-gors –	mountain of the church of the marshland.
Mynydd Llyn Coch-hwyad –	mountain of the lake of the red duck.
Mynydd Llysiau –	mountain of berries
Mynydd Penypistyll –	mountain of the top of the spring or well.
Mynydd Talyglannau –	mountain of the end of the river banks.
Mynydd Waun-fawr –	mountain of the big moor.
Nant Brân –	the Brân river.
Nant-gläs –	blue stream.
Nant-yr-Eira –	sream of the snow.
Nyth y Grug –	nest in the heather.
Pandy –	fulling mill.
Pant-y-Dŵr –	hollow of the water.
Pant-y-ffridd –	hollow of the mountain pasture.
Pen Cerrig Calch –	top of the lime stones.
Pen Coed –	top of the wood.
Pencraig –	top of the rock.
Penffordd-wen –	top of the white roadway.
Pennant –	head of the stream or valley.
Pen-pont –	end of the bridge.
Pen Rhiw-wen –	top of the white hillside.
Pen-rhos –	end of the moorland.
Pentre –	end of the homestead; village.
Pentre-bach –	little village.
Pentrebeirdd –	village of bards.
Pentre'r-felin –	village of the mill.
Pen-y-Begwn –	top of the beacon.
Pen-y-bont-fawr –	top of the big bridge.
Pen-y-cae –	top or end of the field.
Pen y Crocbren –	top of the gallows.
Pen y Crug –	top of the cairn.
Pen-y-fan –	top of the peak.
Pen-y-gaer –	top of the fort.
Pen y Garngoch –	top of the red cairn.
Pontneddfechan –	bridge over the lesser Nedd river.
Rhaeadr Gwy –	waterfall of the Wye river.
Rhos-goch –	red moorland.
Rhos y Gelynnen –	moorland of the holly-tree.
Sarn –	paved way.
Sarnau –	paved ways.

Tafolwern – marsh of dock-leaves.
Talerddig – top of the little garden.
Talgarth – end of the enclosure or headland.
Tal-y-bont – end of the bridge.
Tal-y-cefn – end of the ridge.
Tal-y-llyn – end of the lake.
Tal-y-wern – end of the marsh.
Tarren yr Esgob – the bishop's rock.
Tirabad – land of the abbot.
Tir Rhiwiog – hilly land.
Treberfedd – homestead in the heart of the country.
Tredomen – homestead of the mound.
Tredderwen – homestead of the oak tree.
Trefeca – homestead of Becca.
Trefeglwys – homestead of the church.
Tregastell – homestead of the castle.
Tretŵr – homestead of the tower.
Tre-wern – homestead of the marsh.
Trum y Fawnog – ridge of the peat-bog.
Twmpath Melyn – yellow mound.
Twyn Du – black mound.
Twyn y Gaer – mound of the fort.
Tŷ Crwyn – house of skins.
Tyn-cwm – small holding in the valley.
Waun Fach – little meadow or moor.
Y Bont-faen – the stone bridge.
Y Bontnewydd-ar-Wy – the new bridge on the river Wye.
Y Cribarth – the ridge of a headland.
Y Darren Lwyd – the brown or grey rocky hillside.
Y Drenewydd – the new town.
Y Drum Ddu – the black ridge.
Y Fan Fawr – the long peak.
Y Foel – the bare hill.
Y Ffridd – the mountain pasture.
Y Gamallt – the crooked hillside road.
Y Gamriw – the crooked hillside.
Y Gelli – the grove.
Y Glôg – the rock.
Y Gorllwyn – the large wood.
Y Gribyn – the mountain crest.
Ynys-wen – white island.
Yr Adfa – the border or retreat.
Yr Allt – the wood or hillside.
Yr Arddlîn – the garden of flax.
Yr. Hengoed – the old wood.

Ystradfellte – valley of the river Mellte.
Ystradgynlais – valley of Cynlais.
Y Trallwng – the boggy place.
Y Wennallt – the fair hillside or wood.

X RIVERS, RESERVOIRS AND LAKES

Afon – River

Aeron – fruits or berries (Dyfed).
Aled – a personal name (Clwyd).
Alun – a personal name (Clwyd : Dyfed).
Alwen – a personal name (Clwyd).
Banw – young pig or deer (Powys).
Brân – crow (Dyfed).
Brenig – limpets (Clwyd).
Cain – beautiful; elegant (Gwynedd : Powys).
Camddwr – winding water (Dyfed).
Carno – place of cairns (Powys).
Ceiriog – a personal name (Clwyd).
Ceirw – deer (Clwyd).
Celyn – holly (Gwynedd).
Cennen – a personal name (Dyfed).
Claerwen – clear, bright water (Powys).
Cledwyn – a personal name (Clwyd).
Cletwr – rough water or hard water (Dyfed).
Clydach – a river flowing through a shaded place (Gwent).
Clydach Isaf – lower Clydach (W. Glam).
Clydach Uchaf – upper Clydach (W. Glam).
Clywedog – audible (Powys).
Crai – fresh water (Powys).
Chwefri – wild water (Powys).
Daugleddau – the two Cleddy rivers:
1 Cleddy Ddu (Eastern Cleddy).
2 Cleddy Wen (Western Cleddy). (Dyfed.
Dewi Fawr – the greater river of David (Dyfed)
Di-honnaid – the quiet or unknown water (Powys).
Dugoed – the black wood (Gwynedd-Powys).
Dulais - dark blue (Dyfed : W. Glam).
Dulas – dark blue (Powys: Clwyd : Gwynedd).
Dwyfach – two little ones (Gwynedd).
Dwyfor – two waters (Gwynedd).
Dwyryd – two fords (Gwynedd).

Dyfi –	dark water (Gwynedd).
Dyfrdwy –	the waters of two (Clwyd).
Ddu –	black (Gwynedd).
Eden –	a Biblical name (Gwynedd).
Elan –	a personal name (Powys).
Elwy –	swift water (Clywd).
Ewenni –	frothy water (Mid-Glam).
Ffynnon-groes –	cross-well (Dyfed).
Gam –	crooked river (Powys).
Garw –	rough (Mid-Glam).
Glaslyn –	blue lake (Gwynedd).
Gwaun –	marsh (Dyfed).
Gwendraeth –	white shore (Dyfed).
Gwili –	a personal name (Dyfed).
Gwyrfai –	fresh water (Gwynedd).
Hesgyn –	sieve or riddle (Gwynedd).
Ieithon –	from Ithon – a personal name. (Powys) Ieithon.
Irfon –	a personal name (Powys).
Lliw –	a lake or hollow (Gwynedd : W. Glam).
Llafar –	resounding (Gwynedd).
Llwchwr –	lake water or water from a hollow (Dyfed).
Llwyd –	grey (Gwent : Powys).
Llynfi –	smooth (Powys : Mid-Glam).
Mellte –	swift flowing (Powys).
Mynach –	monk (Dyfed).
Penfro –	end of the land or region (Dyfed).
Porth-llwyd –	grey or brown port (Gwynedd).
Rhaeadr –	waterfall (Clwyd-Powys).
Rhiw –	slope (Powys).
Rhondda –	black hue (Mid-Glam).
Taf –	spreading or expanding (Mid-Glam).
Tawe –	quiet (W. Glam – Powys).
Twrch –	a boar (Dyfed : Powys : Gwynedd).
Twymyn –	feverish (Powys).
Ysgir –	ridge (Powys).
Ystrad –	valley (Clwyd).
Ystwyth –	flexible (Dyfed).

Cronfa – Reservoir

Cronfa Caban-coch –	reservoir of the red cabin or booth (Powys).
Cronfa Cantref –	reservoir of the hundred – an old division of land (Powys).
Cronfa Coed-gwent –	reservoir of the trees of Gwent (Hwent).

Cronfa Crai – reservoir of the river Crai (fresh water) (Powys).

Cronfa Dinas – reservoir of the fort. (Powys).

Cronfa Garreg-ddu – black stones reservoir (Powys).

Cronfa Graig-goch – red rock reservoir (Powys).

Cronfa Isaf y Lliw – the lower Lliw reservoir (W. Glam).

Cronfa Llwyn-onn – ash grove reservoir (Powys).

Cronfa Llys-y-frân – crow's court reservoir (Dyfed).

Cronfa Nant y Moch – reservoir of the stream or valley of pigs (Dyfed).

Cronfa Penygareg – reservoir of the top of the stone (Powys).

Cronfa'r Alaw – the reservoir of the river Alaw (water lily or melody) (Gwynedd).

Cronfa'r Aled-isaf – reservoir of the lower river Aled (a personal name) (Clwyd).

Cronfa'r Alwen – reservoir of the river Alwen (a personal name) (Clwyd).

Cronfa'r Bannau – reservoir of the beacons (Powys).

Cronfa'r Claerwen – reservoir of the river Claerwen (clear, bright water) (Dyfed-Powys).

Cronfa'r Clywedog – reservoir of the river Glywedog (audible) (Powys).

Cronfa'r Neuadd – reservoir of the Hall (Powys).

Cronfa'r Rhondda Fach – reservoir of the lesser river Rhondda (black hue) (Mid-Glam).

Cronfa'r Taf Fechan – reservoir of the lesser river Taf (spreading or expanding) (Powys).

Cronfa'r Wysg – reservoir of the river Wysg (Usk) (Dyfed-Powys).

Cronfa
Tal-y-bont – end of the bridge reservoir (Powys).
Cronfa
Tanygrisiau – below the steps reservoir (Gwynedd).
Cronfa Uchaf
y Lliw – the upper Lliw reservoir (W. Glam).
Cronfa
Ystradfellte – reservoir of the river Meallte (swift) valley (Powys).

Llyn – Lake

Llyn Aled – the river Aled lake (Clwyd).
Llyn Alwen – the river Alwen lake (Clwyd).
Llyn Berwyn – lake of the river Berwyn (foaming) (Dyfed).
Llyn Brân – lake of the river Brân (crow) (Clwyd).
Llyn Cau – hollow or enclosed (Gwynedd).
Llyn Celyn – holly (Gwynedd).
Llyn Cnwch – a small tump (Gwynedd).
Llyn Coch-hwyad – red duck (Powys).
Llyn Coron – crown (Gwynedd).
Llyn Crafnant – stream of the garlic (Gwynedd).
Llyn Dinas – fort or camp (Gwynedd).
Llyn Ebyr – streams or estuaries (Powys).
Llyn Frongoch red-breast (Dyfed).
Llyn Gwynant – white stream (Gwynedd).
Llyn Helyg – willows (Clwyd).
Llyn Hir – long (Powys).
Llyn Hywel – a personal name (Gwynedd).
Llyn Idwal – a personal name (Gwynedd).
Llyn Llech Owen – Owen's slate (Dyfed).
Llyn Mawr – big (Mid-Glam : Powys).
Llyn Morynion – maidens (Gwynedd).
Llynnau Cerrig
Llwydion – the grey stones' lake (Powys).
Llynnau
Duweunydd – lakes of the black meadows (Gwynedd).
Llyn Newydd – new lake (Gwynedd).
Llyn Penmaen – top of the stone (Gwyn).
Llyn Plas-y-
mynydd – mansion of the mountain (Dyfed).
Llyn Trawsfynydd – across the mountain (Gwynedd).
Llyn Y Fan Fach – of the little peak.
Llyn Y Fan Fawr – of the large peak.
Llyn Y Gadair – of the chair.
Llyn Yr Adar – of the birds.
Llyn Y Tarw – of the bull.

APPENDIX
A Welsh-English Glossary of Place Names

Welsh	English
Abaty Tyndyrn –	Tintern Abbey.
Aberafan –	Aberavon.
Aber Bach –	Little Haven.
Abercegin –	Port Penrhyn.
Aberclydach –	Aber Village.
Aber-craf –	Abercrave.
Abercynffig –	Aberkenfig.
Aberdâr –	Aberdare.
Aberdaugleddau –	Milford Haven.
Aberdyfi –	Aberdovey.
Aberddawan –	Aberthaw.
Abergwaun –	Fishguard.
Abergwenffrwd –	Whitebrook.
Aberhonddu –	Brecon.
Aber Llydan –	Broad Haven.
Aberllynfi –	Three Cocks
Aber-miwl –	Abermule.
Abermo –	Barmouth.
Aberogwr –	Ogmore-by-sea.
Aberpennar –	Mountain Ash.
Abertawe –	Swansea.
Aberteifi –	Cardigan.
Abertwymyn –	Cemais Road.
Abertyleri –	Abertillery.
Allteuryn –	Gold Cliff.
Allt Melyd –	Meliden.
Arberth –	Narberth
Argoed –	New Brighton.
Bae Abergwaun –	Fishguard Bay.
Bae Abermo –	Barmouth Bay.
Bae Abertawe –	Fishguard Bay.
Bae Caerfyrddin –	Carmarthen Bay.
Bae Caernarfon –	Caernarvon Bay.
Bae Ceredigion –	Cardigan Bay.
Bae Cinmel –	Kinmel Bay.
Bay Colwyn –	Colwyn Bay.
Bae Conwy –	Conway Bay.
Bae Sant Ffraid –	St. Brides Bay.
Bae Trefdraeth –	Newport Bay.
Bae Tremadog –	Tremadoc Bay.
Banc y Castell –	Castle Bank.
Bangor Is-coed –	Bangor-on-Dee.

Bannau Brycheiniog – Brecon Beacons.
Begeli – Begelly.
Betws Ifan – Bettws Evan.
Biwla – Beulah.
Blaendulais – Seven Sisters.
Bochrwyd – Boughrood.
Borth Uchaf – Upper Borth.
Breudeth – Brawdy.
Bro Morgannwg – Vale of Glamorgan.
Brychdwn – Broughton.
Brynaman-Isaf – Lower Brynaman.
Bryn bach – Little Hill.
Bryn bachell – Bache Hill.
Bryn beili – Bailey Hill.
Brynbuga – Usk.
Bryn Cleirwy – Cyro Hill.
Bryn Coch – Red Hill.
Bryn Colfa – Colva Hill.
Bryn Du – Black Hill.
Bryn Glasgwm – Glasgwm Hill.
Bryn Gwaunceste – Gwaunceste Hill.
Bryniau Ceri – Kerry Hill.
Bryn y Begwn – Beacon Hill.
Bryn y Castell – Castle Hill.
Bwcle – Buckley.
Bwlch Llanberis – Llanberis Pass.
Cadffrwd – Catbrook.
Caehopcyn – Caehopkin.
Caerdydd – Cardiff.
Caerfyrddin – Carmarthen.
Caerffili – Caerphilly.
Caergybi – Holyhead.
Caeriw – Carew.
Caerllion – Caerleon.
Caerllion Fawr – Chester.
Cae'r-onnen – Ashfield.
Cantwn – Canton.
Capel Coed-y-mynach – Monkswood.
Capel Dyffryn Honddu – Upper Chapel.
Capel Newydd – Newchapel.
Capel Tomos – Thomas Chapel.

Carwe –	Carway.
Cas-bach –	Castleton.
Cas-blaidd –	Wolf's castle.
Cas-fuwch –	Castlebythe.
Cas-gwent –	Chepstow.
Cas-haidd –	Hayscastle.
Casllwchwr –	Loughhor.
Cas-mael –	Puncheston.
Casmorys –	Castle Morris.
Casnewydd-ar-Wysg –	Newport.
Casnewydd-bach –	Little Newcastle.
Castell Coch –	Powis Castle.
Castell Gwalchmai –	Walwyn's Castle.
Castell Gwyn –	White Castle.
Castell Gwrych –	Gwrych Castle.
Castell Hendre –	Henry's Moat.
Castell Llangoed –	Llangoed Castle.
Castellmartin –	Castlemartin.
Castell-meirch –	Newcastle.
Castell-nedd –	Neath.
Castellnewydd Emlyn –	Newcastle Emlyn.
Castell Paen –	Painscastle.
Castell Penrhyn –	Penrhyn Castle.
Castell Pictwn –	Picton Castle.
Castell y Waun –	Chirk Castle.
Cas-wis –	Wiston.
Cathonnen –	Cat's Ash.
Cefn Bagillt –	Bagillt Bank.
Cefnbychan –	Newbridge.
Cefn Digoll –	Long Mountain.
Cefn Mostyn –	Mostyn Bank.
Cefn Treffynnon –	Hollywell Bank.
Cegidfa –	Guilsfield.
Ceinewydd –	New Quay.
Cemais – Comawndwr –	Kemeys Commander.
Ceri	Kerry
Cilâ –	Killay.
Cilgeti –	Kilgetty.
Cintwn –	Kinnerton.
Cnwclas –	Knucklas.
Coed-duon –	Blackwood
Coedgolau –	Lightwood Green.

Coed Gwent –	Wentwood.
Coed-llai –	Leeswood.
Coed yr Iarll –	Earlswood Common.
Conwy –	Conway.
Corneli –	Cornelly.
Crai –	Cray.
Craig y Forwyn –	World's End.
Craig y Sger –	Tusker Rock.
Croes Cas-haidd –	Hayscastle Cross.
Crucadarn –	Crickadarn.
Crucywel –	Crickhowell.
Crugiau-Forgan –	Crick.
Cryndâl –	Crundale.
Crynwedd –	Crinow.
Culfor Ddewi –	Ramsey Sound.
Culfor Enlli –	Bardsey Sound.
Culfor Llydan –	Broad Sound.
Cwmbach Llechryd –	Builth Road.
Cwmclydach –	Clydach Vale.
Cwm-Ogwr –	Ogmore Vale.
Cwm Ogwr –	Ogmore Valley.
Cwm Tawe –	Swansea Valley.
Cwrt-henri –	Court Henry.
Cydweli –	Kidwelly.
Cyffordd Llandudno –	Llandudno Junction.
Cynoed –	Kingcoed.
Cynffig –	Kenfig.
Chwitffordd –	Whitford.
Defynnog –	Devynock.
Derwen-gam –	Oakford.
Dinas Basing –	Basingwerk.
Dinas Isaf –	Williamstown.
Dinbych –	Denbigh.
Dinbych-y-pysgod –	Tenby.
Dinefwr –	Dynevor.
Dinorwig –	Dinorwic.
Dolau –	Dolley Green.
Drenewydd –	Newton.
Drenewydd Gelli-farch –	Shiretown
Dulais –	Black Pill.
Eglwys Fair y Mynydd –	St. Mary Hill.

Eglwys Gunniau –	Gumfreston.
Eglwys Wynnio –	St. Twynnells.
Eglwys-Wythwr –	Monington.
Eglwys y Drindod –	Christchurch.
Erbistog –	Erbistock.
Erwdd –	Erwood.
Ewenni –	Ewenny.
Fachelych –	Vachelich.
Faerdre –	Vardre.
Felindre –	Velindre.
Felin-fach –	Little Mill.
Felinganol –	Middle Mill.
Felin-newydd –	Newmills.
Felin-wen –	White Mill.
Froncysylltau –	Vroncysyllte.
Ffontygari –	Font-y-gary.
Ffordun –	Forden.
Ffos Anoddun –	Fairy Glen.
Ffos-y-gerdinen –	Nelson.
Ffwrnais –	Furnace.
Ffynnon Groes –	Crosswell.
Ffynnon Taf –	Taff's well.
Gartholwg –	Church Village.
Gelli-aur –	Golden Grove.
Glan-bad –	Upper Boat.
Glandŵr –	Landore.
Glanyfferi –	Ferryside.
Glynebwy –	Ebbw Vale.
Glyn-nedd –	Glyn Neath.
Groes-ffordd –	Gresford.
Groes-newydd –	New Cross.
Gwaunyterfyn –	Acton.
Gwenfô –	Wenvoe.
Gundy –	Undy.
Helygain –	Halkyn.
Hendy-gwyn (ar-Daf) –	Whitland.
Henllan Didiwg –	Dixton.
Hwlffordd –	Haverfordwest.
Is-coed –	Underwood.
Lecwydd –	Leckwith.
Llanandras –	Presteigne.
Llanarmon –	St. Harmon.
Llanbadrig –	Pembroke Dock.
Llanbedr-ar-fro –	Peterson-super-Ely.
Llanbedr Felffre –	Lampeter Velfrey.

Llan-bedr Gwynllŵg –	Lampeter Wentlooge.
Llanbedr Pont Steffan –	Lampeter.
Llanbydderi –	Llanbethery.
Llan-dawg –	Llandawke.
Llandegfedd–	Llandegvath.
Llandeilo Ferwallt –	Bishopston.
Llandeilo Gresynni –	Llantilio Grossenny.
Llandochau –	Llandough.
Llandudoch –	St. Dogmaels.
Llandudwg –	Tythegston.
Llandyddewi –	St. Dogwells.
Llanddewi Nant Hodni –	Llanthony.
Llanddewi-yn-Hwytyn –	Whitton.
Llanddingad –	Dingestow.
Llanddinol –	Itton.
Llanddunwyd –	Welsh St. Donats.
Llanegwest –	Valle Crucis.
Llaneirwg –	St. Mellons.
Llanelwy –	St. Asaph.
Llaneurgain –	Northop.
Llanfable –	Llanvapley.
Llanfaches –	Llanvaches.
Llanfadog –	Haroldston West.
Llan-fair –	New Hedges.
Llanfair Isgoed –	Llanvair Discoed
Llanfair Llythynwg –	Gladestry.
Llanfair-ym-Muallt –	Builth Wells.
Llanfihangel Dyffryn Arwy –	Michael-church-on-Arrow
Llanfihangel Fechan –	Lower Chapel.
Llanfihangel Troddi –	Mitchell Troy.
Llanfihangel-y-fedw –	Michaelston-y-Vedw.
Llanfihangel-y-pwll –	Michaelston-le-pit.
Llanfocha –	St. Maughan's.
Llangatwg –	Llangattock.

Llangatwg Dyffryn Wysg –	Llangattock nigh Usk.
Llangatwg –	Cadoxton-juxta-Neath.
Llangrallo –	Coychurch.
Llangywer –	Llangower.
Llanhari –	Llanharry.
Llanhenwg –	Llanhennock.
Llanilltud Fawr –	Llantwit Major.
Llanilltud Gŵyr –	Ilston.
Llan-lwy –	Llandeloy.
Llannerch Banna –	Penley.
Llannewydd –	Newchurch.
Llanoronwy –	Rockfield.
Llansanffraid-ar-Elâi –	St. Brides-super-Ely
Llansanffraid Gwynllŵg –	St. Bride's Wentlooge.
Llan San Sior –	St. George.
Llansawel –	Briton Ferry.
Llantrisaint –	Llantrissent.
Llanymddyfri –	Llandovery.
Llan-y-tair-mair –	Knelston.
Llwyncelyn –	Hollybush.
Llwyneliddon –	St. Lythan's.
Llysbedydd –	Bettisfield.
Llys-faen –	Lisvane.
Maenorbŷr –	Manorbier.
Maen y Bugail –	West Mouse.
Maerun –	Marshfield.
Maesaleg –	Bassaleg.
Maes-glâs –	Greenfield.
Maesyfed –	New Radnor.
Marcroes –	Marcross.
Marthan Twyn –	Martletwy.
Meisgyn –	Miskin.
Melin Ifan Ddu –	Blackmill.
Mynachdy –	Monaughty.
Mynwent y Crynwyr –	Quaker's Yard.
Nant-y-fallen –	Bow Street.
Nefyn –	Nevin.
Notais –	Nottage.
Nyfer –	Nevern.
Owrtyn-fadog –	Overton.
Pant-teg –	Pontypool Road.
Penalun –	Penally

Penarlâg –	Hawarden.
Pen Caer –	Strumble Head.
Pen Cemais –	Cemaes Head.
Pencraig –	Old Radnor.
Penfro –	Pembroke.
Penffordd-wen –	Staylittle.
Pengelli –	Grovesend.
Penmaendewi –	St. David's Head.
Penmaenmynach –	Monkstone Point.
Pen Pyrod –	Worm's Head.
Pen Rhos –	St. Ann's Head.
Penrhyn Gŵyr –	Gower Peninsula.
Pen-rhys –	Penrice.
Pentre-elan –	Elan Village.
Pentrefelin –	Milton.
Pentre-ifan –	Evanstown.
Pentre-moch –	Northophall.
Pentre-poeth –	Morganstown.
Pentywyn –	Pendine.
Pen-y-Begwn –	Hay Bluff.
Pen-y-bont ar Ogwr –	Bridgend.
Pen-y-fai –	Paviland.
Penygogarth –	Great Ormes Head.
Pont-ap-Hywel –	Pontypool.
Pontarfynach –	Devils's Bridge.
Pont Fadlen –	Merlin's Bridge.
Pontneddfechan –	Ponteathvaughan.
Pont-rhyd-y-bont –	Four Mile Bridge.
Pontsenni –	Senny Bridge.
Porthaethwy –	Menai Bridge
Porth Llechog –	Bull Bay.
Porth Mawr –	Whitesand Bay.
Porth Neigwl –	Hell's mouth.
Post-mawr –	Synod Inn.
Pump-hewl –	Five Roads.
Pwll-gelen –	Leechpool.
Rhaeadr Ewynnol –	Shallow Falls.
Rhosbwlch –	Rosebush.
Rhos-farcut –	Rosemarket.
Rhos-goch –	Red Roses.
Rhos-hir –	Newborough.
Rhos-yr-hafod –	Cross Inn.
Rhydaman –	Ammanford.
Rhydfach –	Great Rudbaxton.
Rhydri –	Rudry.

Sain Dunwyd –	St. Donat's.
Sain Ffagan –	St. Fagans.
Sain Nicholas –	St. Nicholas.
Sain Siorys –	St. George-super-Ely
Saint Andras –	St. Andrews Major.
Saint Arfan –	St. Arvans.
Sain Tathan –	St. Athan.
Saint-y-brid –	St. Brides Major.
Sancler –	St. Clears.
Sant Ffraid –	St. Brides.
Sili –	Sully.
Silstwn –	Gileston.
Sychdyn –	Soughton.
Tafarnsbyty –	Tavernspite.
Talacharn –	Laugharne.
Tal-y-bont –	Buttington.
Talyllychau –	Talley.
Tonysguboriau –	Talbot Green.
Treamlod –	Ambleston.
Trebefered –	Boverton.
Treberfedd –	Middletown.
Tredegar Newydd –	New Tredegar.
Tredelerch –	Rumney.
Tredeml –	Templeton.
Tredomos –	Thomastown.
Treddraenen –	Thornton.
Trefalaun –	Allington.
Trefarchog –	St. Nicholas.
Trefdraeth –	Newport.
Trefechan –	Trevaughan.
Trefelen –	Bletherston.
Trefonnen –	Nash.
Treforys –	Morriston.
Trefrân –	Newgale.
Trefwrdan –	Jordanston.
Trefynwy –	Monmouth.
Trefflemin –	Flemingston.
Treffynnon –	Holywell.
Tregastell –	Trecastle.
Tregelyn –	Newbridge.
Tregetin –	Keeston.
Tregolwyn –	Colwinston.
Tre-groes –	Whitchurch.
Tre-gŵyr –	Gowerton.
Trelâi –	Ely.
Trelales –	Laleston.

Trelawnyd –	Newmarket.
Treletert –	Letterston.
Trelewelyn –	Leweston.
Treopert –	Granston.
Trericert –	Rickeston.
Tre'r-llai –	Leighton.
Treruffudd –	Griffithstown.
Tresigin –	Siginston.
Tresimwn –	Bonvilston.
Testinan –	Steynton.
Tretŵr –	Tretower.
Trewilym Ddwyreiniol –	East Williamston.
Trewilym Orllewinol –	West Williamston.
Twll Du –	Devil's Kitchen.
Tŷ-du –	Rogerstone.
Tyddewi –	St. David's.
Tyndyrn –	Tintern.
Uwchgwystl –	Four Crosses.
Wrecsam –	Wrexham.
Wyrddymbre –	Worthenbury.
Y Barri –	Barry.
Y Batel –	Battle.
Y Bont Ddu –	Blackbridge.
Y Bont-faen –	Cowbridge.
Y Bontnewydd-ar-Wy –	Newbridge-on-Wye.
Y Bontnewydd-ar-Wysg –	Newbridge-on-Usk.
Y Cerrig –	Bishops and Clerks.
Y Clas-ar-Wy –	Glasbury.
Y Clun –	Clyne.
Y Copa –	Gop Hill.
Y Crwys –	Three Crosses.
Y Cwts –	Wattstown.
Y Drenewydd –	Newtown.
Y Dre Wen –	Whitchurch.
Y Ddwyryd –	Druid.
Y Faenol –	Vaynol Hall.
Y Fali –	Valley.
Y Farteg –	Varteg.
Y Felinheli –	Port Dinorwic.
Y Fenni –	Abergavenny.
Y Ferwig –	Verwick.
Y Friog –	Fairbourne.
Y Garn –	Roch.

Y Gelli –	Hay-on-Wye.
Y Goedwig –	Goodwick.
Y Goetre-Hen –	Coytrehene.
Y Grysmunt –	Grosmont.
Y Maendy –	Maindee.
Y Maerdy –	Mardy.
Ynys Enlli –	Bardsey Island.
Ynys Owen –	Merthyr Vale.
Y Pîl –	Pyle.
Yr Ardro –	Yardro.
Yr Arddlîn –	Arddleen.
Yr As Fach –	Nash.
Yr As Fawr –	Monknash.
Yr Eglwys Lwyd –	Ludchurch.
Yr Eglwys Newydd –	Whitchurch
Y Rhath –	Roath.
Yr Hen Gastell –	Oldcastle.
Yr Hôb –	Hope.
Yr Isga –	Risca.
Yr Oernant –	Horseshoe Pass.
Yr Orsedd Goch –	Rossett.
Yr Wyddgrug –	Mold.
Yr Ystog –	Churchstoke.
Ystrad Fflur –	Strata Florida.
Ystumllwynarth –	Oystermouth.
Y Trallwng –	Welshpool.
Y Tymbl –	Tumble.
Y Waun –	Chirk.

English	**Welsh**
Aberavon –	Aberafan.
Abergavenny –	Y Fenni.
Aberkenfig –	Abercynffig.
Aberthaw –	Aberddawan.
Aber Village –	Aberclydach.
Acton –	Gwaunyterfyn.
Ambleston –	Treamlod.
Ammanford –	Rhydaman.
Ashfield –	Cae'r Onnen.

Bagillt Bank –	Cefn Bagillt.
Bailey Hill –	Bryn Beili.
Bardsey Island –	Ynys Enlli.
Bardsey Sound –	Culfor Enlli.
Barmouth –	Abermo.
Bassaleg –	Maesaleg.
Beacon Hill –	Bryn y Begwn.
Bettisfield –	Llysbedydd.
Bettws Evan –	Betws Ifan.
Beulah –	Biwla.
Bishops and Clerks –	Y Cerrig.
Bishopston –	Llandeilo Ferwallt.
Black Bridge –	Y Bont Ddu.
Black Hill –	Bryn Du.
Blackmill –	Melin Ifan Ddu.
Black Pill –	Dulais.
Blackwood –	Coed-duon.
Bletherston –	Trefelen.
Bonvilston –	Tresimwn.
Boughrood –	Bochrwyd.
Boverton –	Trebefered.
Bow Street –	Nant-y-fallen.
Brawdy –	Breudeth.
Brecon –	Aberhonddu.
Bridgend –	Pen-y-bont ar Ogwr.
Briton Ferry –	Llansawel.
Broad Haven –	Aber Llydan.
Broad Sound –	Culfor Llydan.
Broughton –	Brychdwn.
Buckley –	Bwcle.
Builth Road –	Cwmbach Llechryd.
Builth Wells –	Llanfair-ym-Muallt.
Bull Bay –	Porth Llechog.
Buttington –	Tal-y-bont.
Cadoxton-juxta-Neath –	Llangatwg.
Caerleon –	Caerllion.
Caernarvon Bay –	Bae Caernarfon.
Caerphilly –	Caerffili.
Cardiff –	Caerdydd.
Cardigan –	Aberteifi.
Cardigan Bay –	Bae Ceredigion.
Carew –	Caeriw.
Carmarthen –	Caerfyrddin.

Carmarthen Bay – Bae Caerfyddin.
Carmel Head – Trwyn y Gadair.
Carway – Carwe.
Castle Bank – Banc y Castell.
Castlebythe – Cas-fuwch.
Castle Hill – Bryn y Castell.
Castlemartin – Castellmartin.
Castle Morris – Casmorys.
Castleton – Cas-bach.
Catbrook – Cadffrwd.
Cemaes Head – Pen Cemais.
Cemais Road – Abertwymyn.
Chepstow – Cas-gwent.
Chirk – Y Waun.
Christchurch – Eglwys y Drindod.
Churchstoke – Yr Ystog.
Church Village – Gartholwg.
Clydach Vale – Cwmclydach.
Clyne – Y Clun.
Colva Hill – Bryn Colfa.
Colwinston – Tregolwyn.
Colwyn Bay – Bae Colwyn.
Conway Bay – Bae Conwy.
Cowbridge – Y Bont Faen.
Coychurch – Llangrallo.
Coytrahene – Goetre-hen.
Cray – Crai.
Crickadarn – Crucadarn.
Crickhowell – Crucywel.
Crinow – Crynwedd.
Cross Inn – Rhos-yr-hafod.
Crossway – Groes ffordd.
Crosswell – Ffynnon Groes.
Crumlin – Crymlyn.
Crundale – Cryndâl.
Cwmtillery – Cwmtyleri.
Denbigh – Dinbych.
Devil's Bridge – Pontarfynach.
Devil's Kitchen – Twll Du.
Devynock – Defynnog.
Dinas Head – Pen Dinas.
Dingestow – Llandingad.
Dixton – Henllan Didiwg.
Druid – Y Ddwyryd.
Dynevor – Dinefwr.
Earlswood Common – Coed yr Iarll.

East
Williamstown – Tréwilym Ddwgreiniol.
Ebbw Vale – Glynebwy.
Elan Village – Pentre-elan.
Ely – Trelái.
Evanstown – Pentre-ifan.
Ewenny – Ewenni.
Fairbourne – Y Friog.
Fairy Glen – Ffos Anoddun.
Ferryside – Glanyfferi.
Fishguard – Abergwaun.
Fishguard Bay – Bae Abergwaun.
Five Roads – Pump Hewl.
Flemingston – Trefflemin.
Font-y-gary – Ffontygari.
Forden – Ffordun.
Four Mile Bridge – Pont-rhyd-y-bont.
Frank's Bridge – Pont-ffranc.
Furnace – Ffwrnais.
Gileston – Silstwn.
Glasbury – Y Clas-ar-Wy.
Goldcliff – Allteurin.
Golden Grove – Gelli-aur.
Goodwick – Y Goedwig.
Gop Hill – Y Copa.
Gowerton – Tre-gŵyr.
Great Ormes
Head – Penygogarth.
Great Rudbaxton – Rhydfach.
Greenfield – Maes-glâs.
Gresford – Groes-ffordd.
Griffithstown – Treruffudd.
Grosmont – Y Grysmwnt.
Grovesend – Pengelli.
Guilsfield – Cegidfa.
Gumfreston – Eglwys Gunniau.
Gwaunceste Hill – Bryn Gwaunceste.
Halfway – Y Felindre.
Halkyn – Helygain.
Haroldstown West – Llanfadog.
Haverfordwest – Hwlffordd.
Hawarden – Penarlâg.
Hay Bluff – Pen y Begwn.
Hay-on-Wye – Y Gelli.

Haycastle – Cas-haidd.
Haycastle Cross – Croes Cas-haidd.
Hell's Mouth – Porth Neigwl.
Henry's Moat – Castell Hendre.
Holly Bush – Llwyncelyn.
Holyhead – Caergybi.
Holywell – Treffynnon.
Holywell Bank – Cefn Treffynnon.
Hope – Yr Hôb.
Horeshoe Pass – Yr Oernant.
Ilston – Llanilltud Gŵyr.
Itton – Llanddinol.
Jordanston – Trefwrdan.
Keeston – Tregetin.
Kemeys
Commander – Cemais Comawndwr.
Kenfig – Cynffig.
Kerry – Ceri.
Kidwelly – Cydweli.
Kilgetty – Cilgeti.
Killay – Cilâ.
Kingcoed – Cyncoed.
Kinmel Bay – Bae Cinmel.
Kinnerton – Cintwn.
Knighton Trefyclo.
Knucklas – Cnwclas.
Leleston – Trelales.
Lampeter – Llanbedr Pont Steffan.
Lamphey – Llandyfai.
Landore – Glandŵr.
Laugharne – Talacharn.
Leechpool – Pwll-gelen.
Leeswood – Coed-llai.
Leighton – Tre'r-llai.
Letterston – Treletert.
Leweston – Trelewelyn.
Lightwood Green – Coedgolau.
Lisvane – Llys-faen.
Little Haven – Aber Bach.
Little Hill – Bryn Bach.
Little Mill – Felin-fach.
Little Newcastle – Casnewydd-bach.
Long Mountain – Cefn Digoll.
Loughor – Casllwchwr.
Lower Brynaman – Brynaman Isaf.
Lower Chapel – Llanfihangel Fechan.

Lower Town –	Pentre-isaf.
Ludchurch –	Yr Eglwys Lwyd.
Llanbedr Hill –	Bryn Llanbedr.
Llanberis Pass –	Bwlch Llanberis.
Llanbethery –	Llanbydderi
Llanblethian –	Llanfleiddan.
Llandegveth –	Llanddegfedd.
Llandeloy –	Llan-lwy.
Llandevenny –	Llandyfenni.
Llandogo –	Llaneuddogwy.
Llandough –	Llandochau.
Llandovery –	Llanymddyfri.
Llandudno Junction –	Cyffordd Llandudno.
Llangennith –	Llangynydd.
Llangoed Castle –	Castell Langoed.
Llangunnor –	Llangynnwr.
Llanrumney –	Llanrhymni.
Llantilio Crossenny –	Llandeilo Gresynni.
Llantilio Pertholey –	Llandeilo Bertholau.
Llantrithyd –	Llantriddyd.
Llantwit Major –	Llanilltud Fawr.
Llanfair Discoed –	Llanfair Isgoed.
Llanvetherine –	Llanwytherin.
Llay –	Llai.
Manorbier –	Maenorbŷr.
Mardy –	Y Maerdy.
Marshfield –	Maerun.
Meliden –	Allt Melyd.
Menai Bridge –	Porthaethwy.
Merlin's Bridge –	Pont Fadlen.
Merthr Vale –	Ynysowen.
Michaelchurch-on-Arrow –	Llanfihangel Dyffryn Arwy.
Michaelston-le-Pit –	Llanfihangel-y-pwll.
Michaelston-super-Ely –	Llanfihangel-ar-Elái.
Michaelston-y-Vedw –	Llanfihangel-y-Fedw.
Middle Mill –	Felinganol.
Middletown –	Treberfedd.
Milford Haven –	Aberdaugleddau.

Milton –	Pentrefelin.
Miskin –	Meisgyn.
Mitchel Troy –	Llanifhangel Troddi.
Monaughty –	Mynachdy.
Monington –	Eglwys-wythwr.
Monknash –	Yr As Fawr.
Monkswood –	Capel Coed-y-mynach.
Monmouth –	Trefynwy.
Morganstown –	Pentre-poeth.
Morriston –	Treforys.
Mostyn Bank –	Cefn Mostyn.
Mountain Ash –	Aberpennar.
Moylgrove –	Trewyddel.
Nash –	Yr As Fach (S. Glam).
Nash –	Trefonnen (Gwent).
Neath –	Castell-nedd.
Nelson –	Ffos-y-Gerdinen.
Nevern –	Nyfer.
Nevin –	Nefyn.
Newborough –	Rhos-hir.
Newbridge –	Cefnbychan.
Newbridge on Usk –	Bontnewydd-ar-Wysg.
Newbridge on Wye –	Bontnewydd-ar-Wy.
Newcastle –	Castell-meirch.
Newcastle Emlyn –	Castellnewydd Emlyn.
Newchapel –	Capel Newydd.
Newchurch –	Llannewydd.
New Cross –	Groes-newydd.
Newgate –	Trefrân.
New Hedges –	Llan-fair.
Newmarket –	Trelawnyd.
Newmills –	Felin-newydd.
New Moat –	Y Mot.
Newport –	Casnewydd-ar-Wysg (Gwent).
Newport –	Trefdraeth (Dyfed).
Newport Bay –	Bae Trefdraeth.
New Quay –	Ceinewydd.
New Radnor –	Maesyfed.
Newton –	Drenewydd.
Newtown –	Y Drenewydd.
New Tredegar –	Tredegar Newydd.
Northop –	Llaneurgain.
Northophall –	Pentre-moch.
Nottage –	Notais.
Oakford –	Derwen-gam.

Ogmore-by-sea –	Aberogwr.
Ogmore Vale –	Cwm-ogwr.
Oldcastle –	Yr Hen Gastell.
Old Radnor –	Pencraig.
Oystermouth –	Ystumllwynarth.
Painscastle –	Castell Paen.
Paviland –	Pen-y-fai.
Pembroke –	Penfro.
Pembroke Dock –	Llanbadrig.
Penally –	Penalun.
Pendine –	Pentywyn.
Pendoylan –	Pendeulwyn.
Penley –	Llannerch Banna.
Penrice –	Pen-rhys.
Peterston-super-Ely –	Llanbedr-y-fro.
Peterstone Wentlooge –	Llanbedr Gwynllŵg.
Picton Castle –	Castell Pictwn.
Pontypool –	Pont-y-pŵl.
Port Dinorwic –	Y Felinheli.
Porteynon –	Porth Einon.
Portmadoc –	Porthmadog.
Port Penrhyn –	Abercegin.
Presteigne –	Llanandras.
Puncheston –	Cas-mael.
Pyle –	Y Pîl.
Quakers Yard –	Mynwent y Crynwyr.
Red Hill –	Bryn Coch.
Red Roses –	Rhos Goch.
Rickeston –	Trericert.
Risca –	Yr Isga.
Roath –	Y Rhath.
Roch –	Y Garn.
Rockfield –	Llanoronwy.
Rogerstone –	Tŷ-du.
Rosebush –	Rhosbwlch.
Rosemarket –	Rhosfarcut.
Rossett –	Yr Orsedd Goch.
Rudry –	Rhydri.
St. Andrews Major –	Saint Andras.
St. Arvans –	Saint Arfan.
St. Asaph –	Llanelwy.
St. Athan –	Sain Tathan.
St. Brides –	Sant Ffraid.

St. Brides Bay –	Bae Sant Ffraid.
St. Brides Major –	Saint-y-brid.
St. Bride's-super Ely –	Llansanffraid-ar-Elái.
St. Bride's Wentlooge –	Llansanffraid Gwynllŵg.
St. Clears –	Sancler.
St. David's –	Tyddewi.
St. David's Head –	Penmaendewi.
St. Dogmaels –	Llandudoch.
St. Dogweels –	Llandyddewi.
St. Donat's –	Sain Dunwyd.
St. Fagans –	Sain Ffagan.
St. George –	Llan San Sior.
St. George-super-Ely –	Sain Siorys.
St. Harmon –	Llanarmon.
St. Ishmael's –	Llanismel.
St. Lythan's –	Llwyneliddon.
St. Mary Church –	Llan-fair.
St. Mary Hill –	Eglwys Fair y Mynydd.
St. Maughan's –	Llanfocha.
St. Mellons –	Llaneirwg.
St. Nicholas –	Sain Nicolas (S. Glam).
St. Nicholas –	Trefarchog (Dyfed).
St. Twynnells –	Egwys Wynnio.
Senni Bridge –	Pontsenni.
Seven Sisters –	Blaendulais.
Siginston –	Tresigin.
Sketty –	Sgeti.
Skewen –	Sgiwen.
Soughton –	Sychdyn.
Spittal –	Ysbyty.
Staylittle –	Penffordd-wen.
Steynton –	Trestinan.
Strata Florida)	Ystrad-fflur.
Sully –	Sili.
Swansea –	Abertawe.
Taff's Well –	Ffynnon Taf.
Talbot Green –	Tonysguboriau.
Talley –	Talyllychau.
Templeton –	Tredeml.
Tenby –	Dinbych-y-pysgod.
Thomas Chapel –	Capel Tomos.
Thomastown –	Tretomas.
Thornton –	Treddraenen.

Three Cocks –	Aberllynfi.
Three Crosses –	Y Crwys.
Tintern)	Tyndyrn.
Tintern Abbey –	Abaty Tyndyrn.
Towyn –	Tywyn.
Trecastle –	Tregastell.
Treffgarne –	Trefgarn.
Tregare –	Tre'r-gaer.
Trevaughan –	Trefechan.
Trevine –	Tre-fin.
Tumble –	Y Tymbl.
Tythegston –	Llandudwg.
Underwood –	Is-coed.
Undy –	Gwndy.
Upper Boat –	Glan-bad.
Upper Borth –	Borth Uchaf.
Upper Chapel –	Capel Dyffryn Honddu.
Upper Killay –	Cilâ Uchaf.
Usk –	Brynbuga.
Vachelich –	Fachelych.
Vale of Glamorgan –	Bro Morgannwg.
Valley –	Y Fali.
Vardre –	Faerdre.
Varteg –	Y Farteg.
Velindre –	Felindre.
Verwick –	Y Ferwig.
Vroncysyllte –	Froncysylltau.
Welshpool –	Y Trallwng.
Welsh St. Donats –	Llanddunwyd.
Wentwood. –	Coed Gwent.
Wenvoe –	Gwenfô
West Mouse –	Maen y Bugail.
West Williamston –	Trèwilym Orllewinol.
Whitchurch –	Yr Eglwys Newydd.
Whitebrook –	Abergwenffrwd.
White Castle –	Castell Gwyn.
White Mill –	Felin-wen.
Whitford –	Chwitffordd.
Whitland –	Hendy-gwyn (-ar-Daf).
Whitton –	Llanddewi-yn-Hwytyn.
Williamstown –	Dinas Isaf.
Wiston –	Cas-wis.
Wolf's Castle –	Cas-blaidd.
World's End –	Craig y Forwyn.

Worm's Head – Pen Pyrod.
Worthenbury – Wyrddymbre.
Yspitty – Ysbyty.

Other books in Welsh (or of Welsh interest) from the same publishers:—

English/Welsh; Welsh/English, a phrasebook.
Welsh Words and Phrases.
Getting around in Welsh, a phrasebook.
Learning Welsh, a book for beginners.
First Aid in Welsh.
A Pocket Welsh Dictionary.
Test Yourself in Welsh.
Passport to Wales, a Guide to Basic Welsh.
Welsh Names for Children — Their Meanings Explained.
Welsh Place Names — Their Meanings Explained.